Wevita

From Bones to Thrones

Akhil Rajarathinam

Wevita traces the chain reaction that built the modern world—from fire to farming, villages to cities, myths to institutions. Part thriller, part time machine, it's a page-turning origin story of why life feels like this—and why we're still fighting about it.

Wevita: From Bones to Thrones

(English)

(History)

ISBN Number: 978-93-5692-266-2

Author: Akhil Rajarathinam

First Published: February 2026

About the Author

Akhil Rajarathinam holds a mechanical engineering degree from the University of Kerala. He is an accomplished journalist with work experience across esteemed print and online media. With a fervent passion for India's rich art, culture, and travel, he has covered the length and breadth of the country. He thrives as a skilled Photographer, Vlogger, Writer, Historian, Tutor and is also an India Book of Records holder.

Works by Author

1. Grey Gospels [History | English]
2. Lalama [Poetry | Malayalam]
3. Idavazhiyile Dragon [Travelogue | Malayalam]
4. Dragons in the Alley [Travelogue| English]
5. Indian Art & Culture [History | English]
6. Thenga Talkies [History | English]
7. Kaliyug Kurukshetra [Poetry | English]
8. Local Vocals [Travelogue | English]
9. Bohemian Bodhisattva [Travelogue | English]
10. Kshatra Kshaya [Novel | English]
11. Vilupta Rajya [Drama | English]
12. Bhrasta Dweepu [Drama | Malayalam]
13. Bad Boss Blueprint [Satire | English]
14. Differed Flight, Aligned Might [Non Fiction | English]
15. Ballots, Buffoons and the Big Balagan [Novel | English]
16. The Rebel's Letterbox [Novel | English]
17. Curse of Kumarikandam [Novel | English]
18. Sins & Sermons [Novel | English]
19. Eternal Ebb [Novel | English]
20. Becoming Bharat [History | English]
21. Dharmatattva Ltd [Novel | English]
22. Kaalpa [Novel | English]
23. Utkal Banga [Travelogue | English]
24. Maitreya: The Falling Lotus [Novel | English]
25. Maitreya: The Iron Empire [Novel | English]
26. Maitreya: The Shadow Prophecy [Novel | English]
27. Maitreya: The War of Dawn [Novel | English]
28. The Laugh Sabha [Drama | English]
29. Rattice Reverie [Novel | English]
30. The Demockery [Non Fiction | English]
31. Wevita: From Bones to Thrones [History | English]

CONTENTS

Preface

I've written a lot of words in my life—on deadlines, on roads, in hotel rooms with bad Wi-Fi, in the quiet after a long day when the only honest company is a blinking cursor. Most of them were about *something that just happened*: a festival, a political twist, a place that surprised me, a person who didn't. But this book came from a different itch—older, deeper, and annoyingly persistent.

It's the itch you get when you're standing in a crowded railway station in India, camera strap digging into your neck, watching thousands of lives move in every direction, and you suddenly wonder: **how did we become a species that builds timetables?** How did we go from bones and breath and hunger to tickets, borders, paperwork, empires, ideologies, and that peculiar modern habit of arguing about everything while still needing dinner?

That question followed me everywhere. It followed me through workspaces, conversations, classroom doubts, through long bus rides and short tempers, through temple courtyards and museum corridors, through the sheer, beautiful chaos of travel. I've covered the length and breadth of this country with the instincts of a journalist and the eyes of a photographer—always collecting stories, always trying to understand the *why* beneath the *what*.

And somewhere along the way, I realized something slightly embarrassing: the biggest story I kept circling wasn't one event or one era. It was the whole human arc—the slow, improbable climb from the first managed fire to the first managed state; from foraging minds to bureaucratic minds; from intimate bands to anonymous crowds; from the warmth of a hearth to the cold, glittering logic of thrones.

That's what ***Wevita*** tries to hold. *Wevita* is stitched from two old, simple words—**we** (English, us) and **vita** (Latin, life)—because this story, in the end, is about **our life**.

This is not a book that worships "progress." If anything, it treats progress with suspicion—because history is full of upgrades that come with hidden fees. Farming feeds more mouths and also tightens inequality. Trade spreads ideas and also spreads disease. Writing preserves memory and also enables surveillance. Revolutions promise dignity and sometimes deliver terror. Development lifts millions and still leaves others trapped behind locked gates.

So my goal isn't to hand you a neat ladder of human advancement. My goal is to give you a **map of cause and consequence**—to show how climate, crops, technology, belief, and violence braid together into the world we live inside now. That's why this book moves the way it does: from deep time into early societies, from villages into cities, from rivers into empires, from faith into institutions, from oceans into global systems, from "who rules?" into "who benefits?"

You'll notice another choice I made: I keep returning to scenes. I do that on purpose. Facts matter, dates matter, arguments matter—but **people don't live inside timelines; they live inside moments**. A hearth is not an "innovation." It's warmth against fear. A granary is not a "development." It's tomorrow's hunger negotiated today. A coin is not just currency. It's trust hammered into metal.

Maybe that's the journalist in me. Maybe it's the traveler. Maybe it's also the engineer—because engineering trains you to ask what I think history demands too: *what are the parts, what are the forces, and what happens when you scale the system?*

This book is also personal in another way: I wrote it because I kept meeting readers—especially young ones—who felt history was either a pile of dates or a weapon people use to win arguments. And yes, history can be both. But it can also be something kinder and more useful: a way to recognize patterns, to spot propaganda, to understand why societies repeat mistakes, and to build a little humility into our loud modern certainty.

If a story here challenges what you were taught, sit with it. Check it. Argue with it. History gets stronger under pressure. Names and dates are handles—not the whole object. The bigger question is always: *what changed, and what did that change make possible next?*

A practical note, too: this is an ambitious sweep, and no ambitious sweep is perfect. I've made every effort to be accurate, but the past is vast, sources disagree, and occasional errors can slip in. If you find one, don't treat it like a "gotcha." Treat it like what history always is: a conversation that keeps sharpening itself.

If you're reading this as a student, I hope this book makes the long story feel less intimidating—and more alive. If you're reading as a casual explorer, jump around; follow your hunger. If you're reading as someone exhausted by today's noise, I hope the deeper timeline gives you perspective: our crises are real, but they are not the first storms humans have had to navigate. And if you're reading as a fellow writer, historian, traveler, or chronicler of the human mess—welcome. We're all, in our own ways, trying to answer the same question:

What does it mean that we are the species that remembers?

If these pages do their job, you won't just see where we came from—you'll recognize the gears still turning, and what it might take, finally, to turn them differently.

Akhil Rajarathinam

"The difference in mind between man and the higher animals... is certainly one of degree and not of kind."

– Charles Darwin

Part I

Deep Time & the First Societies (to c. 10,000 BCE)

1

Becoming Us

The ash is thin, almost shy, spread across the cave floor like a memory you could miss if you blinked. In Wonderwerk Cave in South Africa, sunlight doesn't reach far. It fades into cool darkness where the air keeps its secrets for a million years at a time. Yet in that dim zone, archaeologists have found what looks like the quiet residue of a human kind of fire: traces of burned plant material, scorched fragments, heat-touched stone. Not a wildfire that wandered in, but something more intimate and repeated. A hearth, or the early logic of one.

You can imagine the scene without inventing a character. People gather where light can be controlled. Smoke threads upward, leaving its faint signature in the sediment. Meat or tubers warm and soften. The night holds back. Time changes shape. Around fire, a group is no longer only reacting to the world; it is editing it.

That is one doorway into the long story of becoming human. Not a single moment, not a single "first," and certainly not a neat ladder from primitive to modern. It is a deep-time drift of bodies, minds, and relationships, played out mostly in **Africa**, under shifting skies and across landscapes that refused to stay the same.

If you walk the story backward, you don't find an origin point wrapped in myth. You find a widening trail. Around **7 million years ago**, the earliest known hominins appear in the African record, still close to the common ancestor shared with other apes, yet beginning to experiment with new ways of moving and living. By **4.4 million years ago**, fossils like *Ardipithecus* suggest creatures that could walk upright on the ground but still climb well, occupying a world that was not simply forest or savanna but a mosaic of both. Later, between about **4 and 3 million years ago**, australopithecines spread across parts of eastern and southern Africa. Their brains were not large by modern standards, but their bodies were already reshaped around bipedal life. Upright walking is often described as a triumph of efficiency. It is also a bet on a changing world: a way to travel farther, carry more, see above grass, and keep the hands free. Hands matter, because they are where the next revolution becomes visible.

Around **2.6 million years ago** in East Africa, stone tools appear in clear abundance. The earliest widely recognized tradition, often called **Oldowan**, is simple in form and profound in consequence. A hammerstone strikes a core; sharp flakes leap off with edges that slice. With those flakes, you can open a carcass faster than teeth alone. You can strip meat, scrape hides, crack bones for marrow, cut plant fibers. The tool does not merely extend the hand. It changes the diet, and diet changes the body.

This is where "becoming human" stops being only anatomy and becomes ecology. More calories, especially from meat and fat, can support bigger brains over evolutionary time. But the story is not just brain size. It is the social arrangements that make those calories reliably available. Carcasses draw competitors. Hunting and scavenging are risky. A solitary animal can be bullied off a kill; a group can hold ground. Sharing matters, too, because a large kill arrives all at once and rots quickly. Meat creates a problem that generosity can solve. Cooperation is not only moral. It is strategic.

The tools themselves begin to change. Around **1.7 million years ago**, a new stone technology spreads across Africa and beyond: the **Acheulean** tradition, famous for its handaxes. These are not random sharp rocks. They are shaped, symmetrical, planned. A handaxe is a decision made visible in stone: to strike here, then here, to thin the edge, to keep the balance, to anticipate the next blow. Some were used and discarded quickly; others may have served as multipurpose tools carried across distances. Their existence hints at something crucial: not only skill, but teaching.

Watch an experienced knapper at work and you see why. Stone will punish impatience. One wrong strike can ruin the piece. Learning the craft takes time, observation, correction. It is hard to imagine Acheulean skill spreading widely without social learning that is deliberate and sustained. You do not need a written language for that, but you do need communication: gesture, demonstration, shared attention, perhaps vocal signals more complex than alarm calls. You need children who spend long years watching adults, not just racing toward independence.

By roughly **2 million years ago**, the genus *Homo* expands and diversifies. *Homo erectus* (and closely related forms often grouped as *Homo ergaster* in Africa) develops a taller, more humanlike body built for endurance. These humans range widely, and by around **1.8 million years ago** some populations move out of Africa into Eurasia. This is not yet the great "Out of Africa" story of our own species. It is an earlier wave, driven by ecology and opportunity: corridors opening, animals migrating, climates shifting, groups following resources as they always had.

The world they moved through was unstable in the most basic sense. Over the last few million years, ice ages waxed and waned. Rain belts shifted. Lakes expanded and vanished. Forests opened into grasslands, then reclosed. In such a world, flexibility is a survival trait. The line between success and extinction is often the ability to switch strategies without breaking the group.

Fire belongs to that flexibility. The exact timing is contested, because a campfire leaves fragile traces and nature can mimic heat damage.

But by around **a million years ago**, evidence at sites like Wonderwerk suggests that some early humans were using fire in a sustained way. Later, by roughly **400,000–300,000 years ago**, clearer hearths and repeated burning appear at multiple sites, implying more consistent control. Fire changes everything it touches. It extends the day. It hardens wooden tools. It keeps predators wary. And cooking, in particular, may have been transformative: it makes food softer, safer, and more energy-rich, reducing chewing time and increasing calorie return. Cooking is also a social technology. It pulls people into a shared schedule. Raw food can be eaten alone on the move; cooked food invites waiting, guarding, dividing.

If you want to see why language becomes plausible—why it begins to feel necessary—look at a group trying to live by complex foraging in a variable world. They need to coordinate who goes where, when, and with what tools. They need to manage conflicts before they fracture the band. They need to teach skills that take years. They need to negotiate sharing and childcare and risk. No fossil preserves a sentence. But the shape of the lifestyle points toward richer communication, because the alternative is too brittle.

And then, somewhere in Africa, a new kind of human appears.

By about **300,000 years ago**, fossils from places like **Jebel Irhoud** in Morocco are often discussed as early representatives of *Homo sapiens*. The emergence of our species is not a single birth scene. It is a braided process across the continent, with populations mixing and diverging over long periods. What becomes "human" in the modern sense is not just a skull shape. It is a capacity to build worlds inside the world: social networks, shared meanings, symbols that carry identity beyond the moment.

The archaeological record begins to hint at that inner world in ways stone tools alone cannot. Pigments—especially **ochre**, a naturally occurring red mineral—appear at multiple African sites across the Middle Stone Age, sometimes with evidence of grinding and preparation. Red earth can be practical: it can preserve hides, repel insects, protect skin. But it can also be aesthetic and symbolic, because it is visible, deliberate, and hard to explain purely as accident. By around **100,000–70,000 years ago**, the evidence becomes more suggestive still at places like **Blombos Cave** on South Africa's coast, where engraved ochre pieces and shell beads point toward ornamentation and design. An engraving is a mark made for reasons that go beyond immediate survival. A bead is a message worn on the body: about belonging, status, relationship, perhaps belief.

These are not yet the sweeping cave galleries of Ice Age Europe, not yet the famous animals painted in torchlight. But they are the opening notes of the same human ability: to make meaning visible, to store it outside the mind, to let it travel across time. A pigment-stained grinding stone, a crosshatched ochre fragment, a bead drilled and strung. Small objects, heavy implications.

Over millions of years in Africa, hominins become increasingly social, increasingly technological, increasingly dependent on cooperation. Tools are not just things. They are traditions transmitted across generations. Fire is not just heat. It is a social center that reorganizes time and safety. Communication is not just sound. It is coordination, teaching, and trust. Symbols are not just decoration. They are the early architecture of identity.

None of this happens smoothly. Species branch and vanish. Technologies appear, spread, and sometimes disappear. Climate squeezes populations into refuges and then releases them into expansions. What survives is not a straight line of progress but a set of capacities that fit an unpredictable planet.

Return, finally, to that cave floor and the faint ash line pressed into sediment. It is not a banner that says "Here begins humanity." It is quieter than that, and more believable: evidence that people returned to a place, gathered, managed fire, and left traces of a life lived together. The hearth is not the first human act, but it is one of the most revealing. It turns landscape into home, time into shared time, food into a meal.

And once meals exist, once stories can be told around heat and light, the next question arrives almost automatically. What do minds do with the dark beyond the fire? What do they paint onto it, bury into it, sing into it, fear into it?

2

Ice Age Minds

The torch spits and crackles as it bites into the cave air. Smoke gathers in a low ceiling you can't quite see, then slides away into darkness. Somewhere behind the light, water drips steadily, as if the rock is counting time. On the wall ahead, the stone swells and dips like the flank of an animal. A hand follows those curves, not idly, but with purpose. Charcoal smears into a line. Ochre turns the rock warm. A bison's shoulder appears first, then a horn, then the tension in a leg. The painter pauses often, stepping back into the half-light to judge the shape. In the cold world outside, food is never guaranteed. Inside here, something else is being secured: a way of seeing, a way of belonging, a way of carrying knowledge that muscle and appetite alone cannot hold.

Between roughly **50,000 and 12,000 years ago** (a span that reaches from about **48,000 BCE to 10,000 BCE**, with regional variation), much of the Northern Hemisphere sits under a climate that swings hard. Glaciers expand, retreat, expand again. Grasslands replace forests, then forests creep back. Herd animals migrate. Coastlines shift. In such a world, survival depends on more than strength and sharp stone. It depends on information: where the animals will be next season, which valley stays sheltered in a bad winter, which plants return first after a freeze, which group can be trusted, which group will raid you, and how to keep children alive long enough to learn any of this.

Culture becomes that information system. Not as an ornament on top of survival, but as a survival technology in its own right.

You can see it in the objects people carry. A bead necklace seems small compared to a spear point, but in a landscape of strangers, beads can do work a weapon cannot. They can signal who you are, who you are connected to, who will vouch for you, who you might marry, who might share food with you when the hunt fails. Archaeologists find shells far inland, teeth drilled and polished, bits of ivory shaped into pendants, pigments carried and ground. These are not random. They are portable identity, portable memory.

You can see it in the time children take to grow up. Humans do something unusual among primates: we stretch childhood. We stay dependent for years, not months. That is a burden in a harsh climate. It is also an investment. A long childhood only makes sense if the payoff is learning something complex enough to require it. And Ice Age life is complex. It is reading tracks in snow and mud. It is knowing how to stitch hides so clothing becomes insulation rather than decoration. It is learning where to find flint, how to strike it, how to heat-treat it in some regions, how to turn it into blades that can be renewed and repaired. It is knowing stories about places you haven't seen yet because you may need to go there one day.

Culture, in other words, is not only about beauty. It is about training minds to handle uncertainty. That uncertainty is what sits behind the famous images on cave walls. The great painted caves of Ice Age Europe are not simply "art galleries." Many of them are deep, dark, and difficult to access, which makes them strange places to paint if the goal is everyday decoration. **Chauvet-Pont-d'Arc** in what is now southern

France contains images that are tens of thousands of years old, likely around **36,000 years ago** (roughly **34,000 BCE**, though exact dating is complex). Later, caves like **Lascaux** in southwestern France, painted around **17,000 years ago** (about **15,000 BCE**), and **Altamira** in northern Spain, with paintings from broadly similar late Ice Age millennia, show astonishing skill: shading, motion, animals layered over animals as if the wall itself is alive.

It is tempting to take these images as proof of a sudden leap, a "creative explosion" that marks modern humans stepping onto the stage fully formed. For much of the twentieth century, that story was common: a "behavioral revolution" around 50,000 years ago, as if a switch flipped and symbolic thought turned on. But evidence doesn't sit still, and the story has become more complicated.

Long before the European caves were painted, people in Africa were already working with symbols in ways that look deliberate and social. Ochre processing and engraving show up in multiple Middle Stone Age contexts. Shell beads and engraved pieces from sites like **Blombos Cave** in South Africa, often discussed in the range of roughly **100,000–70,000 years ago**, suggest that ornamentation and abstract marking were not inventions of Ice Age Europe. They were capacities developed over long time spans, in different places, with periods of intensification and quiet.

Even in Eurasia, the boundary lines blur. Neanderthals, long portrayed as incapable of symbolism, have left evidence that many scholars interpret as meaningful behavior: use of pigments, possible ornamentation, and signs of care for injured individuals. Some claims remain debated, especially around burials and art attribution, but the direction is clear: the human story is not a clean split between "modern" and "not." It is a spectrum of behaviors emerging unevenly, shaped by population density, environment, and contact between groups.

So instead of asking whether culture appeared "suddenly," a better question is: when did culture become so useful that it spread, intensified, and left unmistakable traces?

The answer may have less to do with a single genetic spark and more to do with a practical reality: in hard environments, small groups are fragile. If a band is isolated and something goes wrong, there is no backup. Culture builds backup.

You can see this in the way networks stretch across landscapes. Stone tools often carry geological fingerprints. A flint blade found in one region can sometimes be traced to a source tens or even hundreds of kilometers away. Sometimes that means people traveled far. Sometimes it means goods moved through chains of exchange. Either way, it hints at a world where groups are not sealed bubbles. They are nodes in a web. The web moves raw material, but it also moves information: who has what, where game is plentiful, which routes are safe, when the salmon run begins, when the reindeer come through.

A web also moves people. Marriage alliances are one of the most powerful technologies humans ever invented. They tie groups together without conquering them. They reduce the risk of conflict. They create obligations that can outlast a bad year. A necklace of familiar beads can be part of that system, a visible sign of affiliation. In the Ice Age, affiliation can be the difference between a hungry winter and survival.

And then there is ritual. Ritual is often misunderstood as irrational. In deep time, ritual can be functional. Shared practices stabilize groups. They synchronize emotions. They create moments when disputes are paused or resolved. They elevate certain rules above daily argument: who belongs, who is protected, who must share, who can marry whom, who can hunt where. In the absence of written law, ritual can be a kind of law written into bodies and memory.

Burials are where ritual becomes most hauntingly visible. Consider **Sunghir** (often spelled Sungir), a site near what is now **Vladimir, Russia**, dated to roughly **34,000 years ago** (around **32,000 BCE**, with uncertainties). There, archaeologists found burials that are hard to explain as practical disposal alone. Individuals were interred with extraordinary quantities of worked ivory beads and other objects, including long spears of mammoth ivory. The labor represented by thousands of beads is immense. Someone had to carve them, drill them, polish them, string them. Then they were placed in the ground, taken out of circulation, offered to the dead.

That choice tells you something about the living. It suggests that some people mattered in ways that were publicly recognized. It suggests that communities could devote time and resources to actions that did not feed anyone directly. In a harsh climate, that is not frivolous. It is a statement: we are the kind of people who honor, remember, and organize ourselves around shared meaning.

Not every burial looks like Sunghir. Many are simple. Some leave no trace at all. But across Ice Age Eurasia, and later across wider regions, burials with grave goods appear often enough to show that humans were increasingly treating death as a social event, not just a biological end. That shift matters. It implies an imagination that extends beyond the immediate present. It implies that the group is larger than the living moment. It includes ancestors, stories, obligations, perhaps spirits. Even if we cannot know exactly what any given group believed, we can see the shape of belief in the actions they took.

Now return to the cave painter. What is being painted? Mostly animals. Not landscapes. Not portraits. Animals that are hunted, feared, admired, or at least obsessively observed. Horses, bison, aurochs, lions, rhinoceroses. The choices themselves are a clue. These images are not random doodles. They are focused attention. They are a record of what matters.

But they are also more than record. The paintings often exploit the natural contours of the rock, turning bulges into shoulders, cracks into movement. They show a mind that can project life into stone. That ability, in other contexts, becomes essential: it is the same mental power that allows humans to plan, to imagine a route across unknown terrain, to conceive of a social rule that isn't visible in nature, to tell a story that binds a group together.

Storytelling is the quiet engine underneath all of this. It is difficult to prove archaeologically, but it is hard to avoid logically. You do not maintain complex social networks, teach intricate skills, and transmit shared symbols without some form of narrative. Stories compress experience. They turn a dangerous ravine into a lesson. They turn an old famine into a warning. They turn a distant group into "kin" or "enemy." They give children a map of the world before they can travel through it.

This is why the "Ice Age mind" is not simply an artistic mind. It is an adaptive mind. The paintings, beads, and burials are not separate categories. They are parts of a system: identity, memory, coordination, and belonging.

And this is where the debates about "behavioral modernity" become more than academic quibbling. If we imagine a sudden moment when humans became "fully human," we miss what the evidence keeps suggesting: modern human behavior appears in pulses, in patches, often earlier than once believed, and sometimes in multiple lineages. Population size and connectivity matter. A small isolated group may have symbolic capacities yet leave few traces. A connected region with more people may produce more artifacts, more innovation, more visible cultural "efflorescence." The difference may not be a mystical threshold. It may be whether ideas can circulate and survive.

The Ice Age, with its pressures and migrations, rewards circulation. When climates swing and resources shift, groups move. When groups move, they meet. When they meet, they exchange not only goods but practices. A better blade technique spreads. A new ornament style appears far from its origin. A ritual pattern changes. A story travels and returns altered. Culture evolves fast because humans are the species that can copy, tweak, and teach at scale.

That has consequences beyond the caves and grave pits. In the short term, culture makes small groups more resilient. It helps them coordinate hunts, share risk, manage conflict, and maintain alliances across distance. It helps them raise children who can master a complex world. It helps them adapt to new ecologies without starting from zero.

In the longer term, culture makes something even larger possible: humans begin to carry their way of life into places they have never been before. They can do that because they can imagine the unseen and teach the unexperienced. They can build portable toolkits of knowledge: how to make fire in a different climate, how to shape clothing for colder winds, how to read coastlines, how to cooperate with strangers, how to keep a group coherent while moving.

Back inside the cave, the torchlight wavers. The painter's work is nearly finished. The animal seems to shift as the flame moves, as if it is breathing. Outside, the wind still bites. The herds still migrate. Winter still comes. But on the wall, the group has placed a kind of anchor: a shared image that can be returned to, remembered, spoken about, argued over, taught to the young.

That is what the Ice Age mind is doing. It is turning culture into a tool that travels. And soon, that tool will carry humans farther than ever—out along coasts, across corridors, onto new continents—until "home" becomes the entire planet.

3

Peopling the Planet

The tide is sliding out, pulling a lace of foam back into the dark water. On the exposed flats, the world suddenly offers itself: shellfish half-buried in sand, crabs scuttling for cover, seaweed glistening like wet hair. A group moves quickly, practiced, silent except for the scrape of tools and the quick, low calls that keep children close. Behind them, the shoreline curves away into haze. Ahead, it continues—always another headland, another bay, another chance to eat.

Nothing about the scene looks like "a great migration." It looks like a day's work. That is the point. Much of humanity's expansion across the planet was not one heroic march but countless ordinary decisions: follow food, follow water, follow familiar corridors. Move when the season says move. Stay when staying makes sense. And when a coastline or a river invites you onward—take the invitation.

By the time our species appears in the African record by roughly **300,000 years ago**, humans are already shaped for mobility: long-distance walking, flexible diets, cooperative childcare, and the cultural toolkits —symbols, shared stories, social bonds—that allow groups to remain coherent even when they split and reunite. But becoming a planetary species required more than legs and curiosity. It required timing. It required corridors opening in the right centuries. It required water levels dropping, climates shifting, and—most crucially—humans learning to treat unfamiliar landscapes as readable.

The phrase "Out of Africa" is often used as if it names a single departure. In reality, it is better understood as a **series of movements** over long spans, some early and limited, some later and world-changing. There were earlier expansions of *Homo erectus* and related humans out of Africa nearly two million years ago, but the global story of **our** species—*Homo sapiens*—takes its decisive shape much later. Many researchers place the major successful dispersal of modern humans beyond Africa somewhere around **70,000–50,000 years ago**, though the exact timing, routes, and number of waves remain debated and continue to be refined as genetics and archaeology improve. What is clear is the direction: over tens of thousands of years, humans spread into environments that ranged from tropical coasts to deserts, from steppe grasslands to ice-edge tundra.

A map of these dispersals would not show a single arrow. It would show branching paths—some hugging the sea, some following rivers, some stalling for centuries, some accelerating when climate allowed. One key question sits at the center of this chapter: did humans mostly move along **coastal routes**, feeding on marine resources and traveling quickly along shorelines, or did they move inland through **river corridors** and grasslands? The answer is likely both, at different times, in different regions, and often in combination. Coastlines offer reliable food and an easy navigational guide: keep the water on one side, and you rarely get lost. Rivers offer the same logic, but inland: water, animals, plant resources, and routes through otherwise harsh landscapes.

Imagine a river-corridor camp somewhere in the Levant or Arabia during a favorable climate window. The river is shallow in places, braided in others. Footprints appear in wet sand and vanish in the next gust of wind. The camp is temporary but organized: a hearth, stone flakes scattered like glitter around a knapping spot, hides stretched, children watched, water carried. People do not need to know a continent's name to move across it. They only need to know what tomorrow's walk looks like, and where the next water is likely to be.

From northeastern Africa, one major gateway outward is the region around the Red Sea and Sinai, linking into the Levant. Another pathway leads through the Arabian Peninsula, especially during wetter phases when deserts were not as forbidding as they are today. These routes matter because they shape not only where humans went, but how often populations met, mixed, or remained isolated. Over time, separation and reconnection leave signatures. Archaeology finds tools and camps. Genetics finds patterns of shared ancestry and divergence. Languages, much later, will also hint at deep histories of movement and separation, though linguistic evidence becomes far clearer in the last several thousand years than in the deep Ice Age.

Now follow the expansion eastward into South and Southeast Asia. Here, the coastal possibility becomes especially vivid. Shorelines are larders. They provide shellfish, fish, sea mammals, and seaweed—resources that can support movement even when inland hunting is uncertain. During Ice Age periods when sea levels were lower, the geography of Southeast Asia changed dramatically. Mainland and islands that are separated today were connected into larger landmasses. But there was still a hard barrier: to reach **Australia and New Guinea**—then joined in a larger landmass often called **Sahul**—humans had to cross open water from **Sunda** (the Ice Age landmass that joined much of mainland Southeast Asia with western Indonesian islands). No land bridge completed the journey. That means boats or rafts, navigation, planning, and social cooperation strong enough to risk a crossing you cannot "undo" once you commit.

By at least **50,000 years ago**, and possibly earlier depending on ongoing debates and new finds, humans are in Sahul. The exact earliest dates in Australia continue to be researched and argued, but the broader fact is solid: reaching Australia requires intentional seafaring. Picture the tools: not grand ships, but practical watercraft—rafts of lashed logs or reeds, perhaps, or dugout canoes in later periods. Imagine stone tools wrapped in fiber, water skins or gourds carried, embers protected to restart fire on the far shore.

The crossing is not a mythic leap. It is a calculated risk taken by people who understand tides, currents, and the simple truth that the sea does not care whether you are brave.

When they arrive, they enter a world of unfamiliar animals and ecologies. The adaptation required is immense: new hunting strategies, new plant knowledge, new seasonal rhythms. Cultural flexibility becomes survival. This is how peopling works everywhere: movement followed by reinvention.

Now turn north and east, toward the Americas—the most dramatic of the late Ice Age expansions, and the most debated in its details.

For much of the twentieth century, the dominant story held that humans entered the Americas late, around **13,500 years ago**, through an inland corridor after ice sheets retreated, associated with the **Clovis** tool tradition. In recent decades, evidence has pushed many scholars to accept earlier presence in at least some parts of the Americas, though the exact timing, routes, and number of migrations remain subjects of active research. What has changed is not just a date but a mindset: the Americas are no longer seen as a last-minute stage. They are recognized as part of a complex, earlier human story.

Two broad routes are often discussed. One is the **inland corridor**: as glaciers retreated in North America near the end of the last Ice Age, a pathway may have opened that allowed movement southward from Beringia into interior lands. The other is the **coastal route**: humans moving along the Pacific rim, perhaps using boats, exploiting marine resources, traveling where the edge of land meets water. The coastal route is hard to prove because sea levels rose dramatically after the Ice Age, drowning many ancient shorelines and the camps that would have sat on them. The evidence may literally be underwater.

But whether by coast, corridor, or a mixture of both, humans adapt quickly once they enter the Americas. They move into deserts, forests, plains, mountains. They learn new animals and plants. They build new social worlds. Over time, their presence reshapes landscapes and is entwined—alongside climate changes—in the stories of megafauna decline and extinction.

Across all these migrations, one pattern repeats: humans do not spread as a uniform wave. They spread as networks that split and reconnect. A small group might push into new territory and then remain isolated for centuries. Another might serve as a bridge between regions, exchanging partners, tools, and knowledge. Over thousands of years, those patterns leave traces in DNA—shared markers, bottlenecks, mixtures—while archaeology captures moments: a hearth, a tool scatter, a shell midden, a campsite along a river bend.

This is where "genetic clues" become part of the story, not as a replacement for archaeology but as another kind of evidence. Genetics can suggest relationships between populations, estimate broad timings of divergence, and reveal episodes of mixing. It can also complicate simple narratives by showing that the past was rarely clean. People moved, met, intermarried, and moved again. A line on a map is never the whole truth.

Language is trickier at this scale. Spoken tongues change quickly relative to tens of thousands of years, and writing arrives far too late to capture Ice Age speech. But the logic of language still matters. Wherever humans went, they carried the ability to teach complex skills, coordinate, and bind groups together through shared meaning. That capacity is part of what made long-distance dispersal possible. A shoreline foraging strategy is not just a set of actions. It is a learned tradition. A sea crossing is not just courage. It is planning shared across a group. A river-corridor route is not just geography. It is knowledge preserved in stories and practice—where water is, where danger lies, what to do when the season turns wrong.

If you want a single image to hold this chapter, keep the shoreline foragers in mind. They are not marching to "settle the world." They are feeding a family, staying near reliable resources, making one choice after another. Those choices add up. A headland passed becomes a new territory known. A river followed becomes a corridor remembered. A successful crossing becomes a precedent. A story about a place becomes a reason to go there—or avoid it.

And somewhere far back in the chain, someone makes a tool not for hunting or cutting, but for travel itself: a binding fiber twisted tight, a waterproofed container, a paddle shaped by careful strikes. It is easy to overlook such objects because they rot and disappear. Yet they are among the most consequential technologies humans ever created. They turn geography from a boundary into an option.

When the tide comes back in, it erases the footprints on the flats. The sea hides evidence as efficiently as it provides food. But the movement continues anyway, guided by coastlines, rivers, seasons, and the human ability to carry knowledge beyond the horizon.

And the horizon is about to get colder. As the planet's climate whipsaws, people will not only move—they will have to survive rapid shifts in where life can be lived at all.

4

Glacial Worlds

The wind has teeth. It comes off the open plain in steady pressure, flattening grass and pulling heat from skin as if it were a resource to be stolen. The shelter is low, hunched against the weather, built from what the world has made abundant: bone, hide, and patience. A curve of mammoth ribs arches into the ground. Skulls—heavy, pale, unmistakable—anchor the frame like stones in a land that offers few stones. Hides are stretched tight and weighted, stitched where they tear, patched where they thin. Inside, the light is a small, controlled thing. Outside, the horizon is endless.

This is one way to live in an Ice Age: not as a tragic struggle against nature, but as a practiced negotiation with it. By the time humans spread across continents, they were not fragile newcomers. They were already experts at adaptation. Yet the world they moved through between roughly **70,000 and 12,000 years ago** was not stable ground beneath their feet. It was a planet that kept shifting its rules.

The most dramatic phase of that instability is known as the **Last Glacial Maximum**, usually dated broadly to around **26,500–19,000 years ago**. During these millennia, ice sheets expanded across northern North America and northern Eurasia. Sea levels dropped by more than a hundred meters compared to today, exposing vast continental shelves and changing coastlines into different worlds. Much of northern Europe was ice or tundra-steppe. Large parts of the Northern Hemisphere became a cold, dry domain where wind and dust could travel far and grow loud.

But the Ice Age was never one uniform climate. It was a patchwork, and the patches mattered. Even at the height of glaciation, pockets of more livable land remained—**refugia**, places where plants, animals, and people could persist when surrounding regions grew harsher. In

Europe, these refuges are often discussed in the south and along certain corridors: parts of the **Iberian Peninsula**, **Italy**, the **Balkans**, and other sheltered zones where ice did not dominate. In Eurasia, refugia were not only Mediterranean; they also existed in steppe-tundra regions where game was plentiful and people learned the rhythms of cold. In other parts of the world, refugia took different forms: river valleys, coasts buffered by the sea, highlands with varied microclimates. The essential point is simple. When climates swing, survival often depends on finding places where the swing is softened.

This reshapes where people live. It also reshapes how they live. Think again of the mammoth-bone shelter. It speaks to a landscape where wood is scarce, where fuel is precious, where winter is not a season so much as a governing fact. In parts of Ice Age eastern Europe, sites such as **Mezhyrich** (in present-day Ukraine), dating to the late Ice Age, have produced famous remains of dwellings built from mammoth bones and covered with hides. Not every group lived this way, and not every site preserves such structures. Bone architecture is partly a gift of preservation and partly a sign of local conditions. But its existence makes something clear: humans did not merely endure the Ice Age. They engineered ways to inhabit it.

Engineering begins with clothing, and clothing rarely survives. Yet the indirect evidence is hard to ignore. People expanded into latitudes where naked skin would be a death sentence. That implies tailored garments, layered insulation, and technologies of stitching. Bone needles and awls show up in many late Ice Age contexts. A needle is a quiet revolution: it allows fitted clothing, which allows deep-cold survival, which opens new territories, which changes the map of humanity.

Engineering also shows up in timekeeping—not clocks, but calendars of attention. When food is seasonal, the mind becomes a schedule. People learn when herds migrate, when rivers run thick with fish, when plants become edible, when ice becomes safe or treacherous. Imagine a seasonal hunting calendar not written on paper but held in a group's routines: the weeks of stalking, the weeks of waiting, the weeks of processing meat into forms that last. A successful hunt is not only killing. It is butchering fast in the cold, drying or smoking strips, storing fat, guarding food from scavengers, dividing shares in ways that keep the group from splintering. That division is not just generosity. It is resilience.

In stable climates, small groups can survive on local knowledge and short-range movement. In unstable climates, resilience favors broader toolkits. Some groups specialize intensely in big game, tracking herds across open steppe. Others broaden their diets, mixing hunting with fishing, shellfish gathering, plant foods, and small animals. The old stereotype of Ice Age people living only by mammoth steaks is too simple. Across regions, foraging economies diversify because diversity buffers risk. If one resource fails, another might hold.

Coasts become particularly important in many places because the sea is a stabilizer. It does not eliminate danger, but it can provide reliable food. Shellfish, fish, sea mammals, seabirds, kelp—these form an edible boundary that can sustain movement and settlement when inland game fluctuates. Rivers do something similar inland. They are corridors of water and life, places where fish runs and waterfowl migrations can be predicted even when rainfall becomes uncertain.

At the edge of ice, the logic sharpens. Ice sheets do not only block movement; they also create ecosystems along their margins. Meltwater streams, cold-rich seas, seasonal concentrations of fish and marine mammals—these can support people who know how to exploit them. Picture ice-edge fishing: not romantic, not tidy, but methodical. The air is sharp enough to sting lungs. The water is black and heavy. People watch the surface and the birds, reading signals that the eye learns only through experience. They cut holes where ice allows, set traps, use lines or spears, and pull life from a place that looks empty to the untrained. This is a different kind of hunting, one that depends on timing and knowledge as much as strength.

All of these strategies—big-game pursuit, broad-spectrum foraging, coastal harvesting, river fishing, ice-edge exploitation—belong to one central reality: the Ice Age rewards flexible minds and cooperative groups. It is not only about tools. It is about social organization. In harsh conditions, isolation can kill. Networks can save.

This is where refugia become more than geography. They become social hubs. When climates worsen, people concentrate into survivable zones. Concentration increases encounters: trade, intermarriage, conflict, alliance. Over time, these hubs can become engines of cultural change. Ideas spread faster when people meet more often. Techniques circulate. Styles of ornament shift. Ritual practices change. The "Ice Age minds" shaped by these pressures. Symbols and social ties are not luxuries. They are the glue that holds networks together across uncertain years.

Climate swings also shape the fate of the great animals—the **megafauna**—that loom so large in Ice Age imagination. Mammoths, woolly rhinoceroses, giant deer, and many other large species thrived in certain glacial environments. But as climates warmed and habitats changed near the end of the last Ice Age, many of these animals declined. In some regions, human hunting pressure likely mattered; in others, habitat loss and rapid ecological shifts may have been decisive; in many places, it was probably a mix. The timing differs by continent and species, and scholars still argue over how to weigh each factor.

The pattern is clearest in its human consequence: when big animals disappear or thin out, people do not stop being human. They adjust. They intensify fishing. They hunt smaller game. They gather more plant foods. They rely more on storage. They rework social rules for sharing and access to key places. In some landscapes, the loss of megafauna removes not only meat but materials—bone, hide, fat—that were integrated into toolkits and shelter. A mammoth-bone dwelling is not only architecture. It is a sign of an ecosystem where mammoths existed in sufficient numbers to be part of daily engineering.

In Australia and parts of the Americas, megafauna extinctions have their own controversial timelines and debates, often intertwined with the arrival of humans and periods of rapid climate change. The arguments can become heated because the stakes feel moral as well as scientific. But deep time rarely offers clean villains. What it offers is complexity: multiple pressures converging on large animals that reproduce slowly and require stable habitats. When the climate changes quickly and humans add new hunting strategies and landscape impacts, the margin for survival narrows.

The most important takeaway is not simply that extinctions happened. It is that Ice Age worlds were dynamic systems, and humans were becoming a dynamic force within them.

As the Last Glacial Maximum eased after **19,000 years ago**, the world did not simply "improve." It transformed. Ice retreated, but meltwater reshaped rivers. Sea levels rose, drowning old shorelines and erasing camps that once sat on exposed coastal plains. Forests returned in some places, changing which animals thrived and how people hunted. In northern regions, entirely new opportunities and dangers appeared as landscapes opened, closed, and opened again. People followed. People adapted. People remembered.

This is what it means to live through deep climate swings without agriculture, without cities, without written forecasts. You build resilience out of portable technologies and social intelligence. You develop toolkits that can be repaired and reconfigured. You learn to store food, share risk, and move without losing the group. You keep networks alive so that when one valley fails, another might help. You hold time in your head as a calendar of migrations and seasons. You turn knowledge into survival.

Back in the mammoth-bone shelter, the wind still scrapes at the hide. The fire is small, protected, carefully fed. Outside, the plain looks empty until you know how to read it: a line of tracks, a shift in bird flight, a distant darkening that might be a herd. The people inside are not waiting for the Ice Age to end. They are living inside it, shaping a life that fits its rules.

And then the rules begin to change faster. Ice melts. Seas rise. Animals vanish or move. Familiar routes transform. The planet becomes more crowded with humans, and human choices begin to matter more. Those pressures will push some groups toward an experiment that will be as consequential as fire once was: settling down, storing more, and reshaping landscapes in ways that make new kinds of society possible.

5

Settling Down

The air smells of smoke and roasted meat, heavy enough to cling to hair and hide. In the half-dark of a large gathering place, firelight flickers over faces and hands and bowls passed from one circle to another. Outside, night presses in, and the wind still carries a cold edge—this is the world after the Ice Age's peak, not yet the gentle climate people will later take for granted. But inside the ring of light, the mood is different from a small camp's quiet discipline. It is loud. It is crowded. It is deliberate. People have walked for days to be here, following paths they know by stories as much as by landmarks. They have come with gifts—meat, grain, shells, stone—and with expectations. A feast is not only food. It is a negotiation.

For most of human history, the dominant rhythm is movement. You go where the animals go, where plants ripen, where water holds. Yet toward the end of the last Ice Age and into the early Holocene—roughly **15,000 to 10,000 BCE,** varying by region—something subtle begins to happen in multiple places. Some communities begin to stay longer in one place. Not forever, not necessarily year-round at first, but long enough to leave deeper traces: heavier houses, storage pits, repeated rebuilding on the same spot. In a few cases, they gather in numbers that feel almost urban compared to older bands. And they build things that are hard to explain as purely practical—monuments, carved stones, arranged spaces meant to hold people's attention.

This is not the story of farming yet. It is the story of the steps before farming, the experiments that make farming possible and, in some regions, make it attractive.

The underlying force is intensification. As the climate warms after the **Last Glacial Maximum** and becomes more stable in many regions, ecosystems reorganize. Forests spread in some places, grasslands shift in others, and plant foods become more predictable. Human populations, already widespread after the dispersals, likely grow in many regions. More people in a landscape changes the math of movement. You cannot simply "move away" from competition if everyone else is also moving, if familiar refuges are already occupied, if the richest hunting grounds are contested. The world becomes more crowded—not densely packed by modern standards, but crowded enough that the old freedom of limitless space begins to narrow.

In such conditions, staying put can begin to make sense, especially in places where resources cluster seasonally or reliably. River valleys, lake shores, rich coastal zones, and ecotones where different habitats meet can provide repeated abundance. If you can harvest a concentrated resource—fish runs, shellfish beds, stands of wild grain—you can support larger groups for longer periods without farming. But this creates another problem: when food arrives in bursts, you need a way to bridge time. You need storage.

Imagine a granary before agriculture. It is not a barn filled with domesticated wheat; it is a sheltered cache of gathered seeds, nuts, dried meat, smoked fish, stored in pits, baskets, or purpose-built structures. Storage changes behavior because it changes incentives. If you have food saved, you can afford to stay. If you stay, you can build heavier structures. If you build heavier structures, you invest more in place. And when you invest in place, you need rules about who belongs, who owns what, and who is responsible for maintaining shared resources.

Sedentism is not a switch. It is a spectrum. Many groups remain mobile while adding seasonal home bases. Others become semi-sedentary, returning to the same location year after year, rebuilding, expanding, accumulating objects that would be burdensome to carry constantly. The archaeology of this transition often looks like layers: repeated floors, hearths built over older hearths, middens that grow into hills, evidence of long-term occupancy. In parts of the Levant, for example, late Ice Age communities associated with what archaeologists call the **Natufian** period (roughly **12,500–9,500 BCE**) show signs of longer-term settlement before full agriculture. They hunted gazelle and gathered wild grains; they lived in more substantial structures than earlier foragers typically did; they buried their dead near their homes, tying identity to place.

Place is the quiet revolution. Once a community sees a location as "ours" in a deep way, the human story changes.

And then there is feasting. Feasting sounds like pleasure, but in deep time it is also politics. A communal feast can be a way to create alliances, to settle tensions, to announce status, to redistribute food, to obligate others through generosity. It can also function as a magnet that pulls dispersed groups into periodic gatherings. Those gatherings matter because they allow traditions to spread and innovations to circulate. They allow marriages to be arranged. They allow disputes to be mediated. They also allow leaders—whether shamans, elders, or skilled organizers—to demonstrate power without permanent coercion.

If you want to understand why monumentality appears before farming in some places, start here. A large gathering creates a need for shared spaces—ritual centers, plazas, structures that mark the occasion and the community's identity. When people return repeatedly, those spaces can grow in ambition. And in certain moments, ambition becomes stone.

Picture a carved pillar site. The stone is pale in the sun, newly quarried, dragged with ropes and coordinated labor. The pillars are too heavy for a single family to raise. Their surfaces are worked with images—animals, symbols, shapes that likely mattered to the people who carved them even if we cannot decode every meaning now. One of the most famous examples of such early monumentality is **Göbekli Tepe** in southeastern Anatolia (modern Turkey), typically dated to around the **10th millennium BCE** (roughly **9600–8200 BCE** for major phases). Here, T-shaped stone pillars arranged in circular enclosures were erected by communities that—so far as current evidence suggests—were not yet fully agricultural in the later village-farming sense. They were hunter-gatherers or complex foragers with access to rich resources, capable of organizing large labor projects.

The significance is not that Göbekli Tepe "caused" farming, as if monuments forced people to domesticate wheat to feed construction crews. The significance is that it breaks simplistic assumptions. It shows that large-scale cooperation, ritual architecture, and social complexity are not exclusive products of agriculture. They can emerge when resources, population, and social networks align in ways that make gathering and organizing worthwhile.

Now place Göbekli Tepe back into a broader world. Across different regions, people are experimenting with new balances between movement and staying. In Japan, early pottery appears among foragers long before agriculture, suggesting that some groups had enough stability—often tied to rich aquatic resources—to invest in heavier technologies. In parts of North America, abundant fisheries and seasonal harvests support semi-sedentary patterns in later periods. Along coasts and river valleys globally, people find ways to thicken their relationship with place.

These experiments come with tensions. Storage invites inequality because stored food can be controlled. If one household guards the granary, or if one lineage claims certain stands of grain or fishing spots, then access becomes political. Sedentary life also concentrates waste and disease, creating health challenges that mobile groups can sometimes avoid. And when people stay, conflict can become more intense, because leaving is no longer the default solution. Boundaries become sharper: this is our place, those are our resources, this is our dead in the ground.

Yet the appeal remains powerful. Staying longer allows deeper knowledge of a landscape. It allows investment in architecture. It allows social institutions—rituals, councils, rules of sharing—to harden into traditions that can hold bigger populations together. It allows children to grow up in environments where learning can be more specialized, where elders can transmit complex knowledge without constant movement interrupting the chain.

In the short term, the consequences are visible in the archaeological record as heavier footprints: more substantial dwellings, storage features, repeated occupation, ritual centers. The social world begins to thicken. People start to live not just in bands but in communities with recognizable identities tied to places and practices.

In the longer term, the consequences are even larger. Once people learn how to stay in one place for long periods, they begin to change the local ecology more significantly—through repeated harvesting, selective gathering, burning practices, and the management of favored species. They begin to shape plant communities, sometimes unintentionally. The boundary between "wild" and "managed" begins to blur. And when that boundary blurs, domestication becomes less like a sudden invention and more like a continuation of practices already underway.

Return to the feast. The fire has burned down to glowing coals. Bones are piled where dogs or scavengers will later nose through them. People talk—about the hunt, about the weather, about who owes what, about who belongs with whom. Someone gestures toward the new structure, the carved stone that will remain when the rest is gone. It is a marker that says: we were here together, and we will be here again.

That expectation—return, rebuild, return—changes everything.

And then, the most consequential experiment begins to spread across multiple parts of the world: the deliberate cultivation of plants and the management of animals, not as a rare supplement but as a new foundation. Farming will not arrive as a single "revolution." It will arrive as many beginnings—each rooted in the long, half-hidden shift that started here, when some people decided that staying put could be worth the risk.

Part II

Farming, Villages & First Monuments (c. 10,000–3500 BCE)

6

Seeds That Changed Us

At the edge of a camp, where the ground has been cleared and trampled flat by many feet, someone kneels with a basket of seed. The seeds are small, pale, easy to spill and impossible to count without losing your mind. They are the kind of food you once gathered when it happened to be ripe, when the grasses were generous, when the season allowed it. Now they are being handled differently. Not as a windfall, but as an asset.

The hand pauses over the pile. Some seeds are bigger, plumper, less likely to shatter. Some stalks stood longer before dropping their grain. Someone noticed. Someone remembered. Someone kept a portion aside rather than eating it. In deep time, that choice is quiet. It doesn't sound like a revolution. It sounds like prudence.

If you could rewind the planet to the end of the last Ice Age, you would not see farmers suddenly replacing foragers as if one way of life "won." You would see something more human and more complicated: communities experimenting. Some tried cultivation and stepped back. Some mixed strategies for centuries. Some never farmed at all and built rich, stable lives by fishing, hunting, and gathering. And in several places, at different times, people moved from managing wild resources to shaping them—deliberately and repeatedly—until the landscape itself began to change. Agriculture did not begin once. It began many times, for many reasons, in many ecologies.

The climate sets the stage. After the coldest millennia of the Last Glacial Maximum, the world warms into the early Holocene, beginning around **11,700 years ago** (roughly **9700 BCE**). In many regions, seasons become more predictable. Rain belts shift. Forests expand in some places, retreat in others. Lakes rise and fall. Familiar animals change routes. Some communities, already experimenting with longer stays and storage as in the previous chapter, find themselves in landscapes that reward deeper investment in place. Others face growing population pressure and competition for rich zones. In either case, the logic tightens: if you can make your food supply more reliable, you lower the odds that a bad year becomes a catastrophe.

But "reliable" can be achieved in more than one way. Along coasts, reliability might mean fish runs and shellfish beds. Along rivers, it might mean aquatic plants and floodplain abundance. In grasslands and woodlands, it might mean intensifying hunting and gathering while building storage and social networks. Cultivation is one answer among several. It becomes a dominant answer in certain regions when plants and animals with the right traits meet humans with the right pressures and the right knowledge.

In **Southwest Asia**, the story is often told first because the evidence is rich and the consequences are enormous. In the broad zone sometimes called the **Fertile Crescent**—stretching through the Levant, northern Mesopotamia, and parts of Anatolia and the Zagros—people had long gathered wild cereals and pulses. By the time you reach roughly **10,000–8500 BCE**, many communities are living in settled or semi-settled villages and storing food. In this setting, cultivation begins to harden into dependence. Wild wheat and barley, lentils and peas, are harvested, sown, tended, and increasingly shaped by human selection. The changes are subtle at first: grains that cling to the stalk rather than shattering and scattering in the wind, seeds that germinate in disturbed soil near settlements, plants that thrive when humans clear competing vegetation.

No one wakes up and declares, "Today we invent agriculture." People simply keep doing what works, and the world responds. Over generations, the plants change in ways that make them easier to harvest and harder to survive without humans. Domestication is not only humans controlling nature. It is nature adjusting to humans.

At the same time, animals begin to move into human social space in new ways. In the hills and margins where wild sheep and goats roam, people start managing herds—first through selective hunting and corralling, then through breeding decisions that favor docility and predictable reproduction. Picture a herder's seasonal route: up to higher grazing in one season, down toward shelter and water in another. The herd becomes moving storage, a living bank account. Animals provide meat, hides, bone, and eventually milk. They also demand labor, vigilance, and new forms of conflict. A herd can be stolen. A grazing territory can be disputed. A mobile wealth can be a reason for war.

This is one origin story. It is not the origin story. Travel east and the logic reshapes itself.

In **China**, domestication emerges along more than one river system and under more than one ecological demand. In the north, around the Yellow River region, **millets**—hardy, fast-growing grasses—become central. In the south, along the Yangtze and its associated wetlands, **rice** becomes the plant that invites deeper investment. Broadly speaking, millet domestication is often discussed in the range of **8000–6000 BCE**, and rice domestication in a similar early Holocene span, though exact dates and processes are debated and vary by site. The important point is not a single year. It is that different plants encouraged different kinds of societies.

Millet thrives in drier conditions and shorter growing seasons. Rice, especially when cultivated in wetlands, encourages careful water control and intensive labor. In one region, fields may be relatively flexible and shifting. In another, water management pulls communities toward coordinated work and long-term landscape engineering. Two agricultural beginnings, in the same broad civilization zone, with different ecological rhythms shaping different social rhythms.

Now move to a place that breaks another common assumption: that farming requires grains.

In the **New Guinea highlands**, people cultivated root crops and bananas in ways that appear early, perhaps by **7000–5000 BCE** or even earlier in some interpretations, with ongoing debates about the evidence and what counts as "domestication" versus intensive cultivation. Here the "garden plot turned field" doesn't begin as a wheat field. It begins as managed earth—ditches, mounds, planting beds—designed for plants like taro and yam. In a wet, mountainous environment, grain agriculture is not the obvious solution. Horticulture is.

Imagine the transformation: a patch of forest cleared, then kept open; soil turned and planted; drainage improved; favored plants replanted from cuttings. The work is incremental, repeated, local. It doesn't always produce surplus in the cereal sense, but it produces reliability. It makes a household less dependent on unpredictable foraging returns. It anchors people to place in a different way, with different crops and different vulnerabilities.

Westward across Africa, another independent beginning grows out of savanna and seasonal uncertainty.

In the **Sahel**—the broad belt south of the Sahara—people develop agricultural systems suited to variable rainfall. Crops like **pearl millet** and **sorghum** become important, with domestication often discussed later than Southwest Asia or China, frequently in the range of roughly **3000–2000 BCE** for key developments, though timelines vary and continue to be refined. What matters is why it happens. In semi-arid zones, farming is a gamble. Yet it can also be a hedge against other gambles: shifting rainfall, changing grazing patterns, and, over time, the long-term greening and drying cycles that reshape where life can be lived.

The Sahel's story is not only farming. It is also mobility. Pastoralism—herding animals across wide landscapes—fits the ecology of grass and seasonal water. Here, the herder's route is not a side note. It is a central institution. Herding and farming intertwine and compete. In good years, animals flourish. In bad years, stored grain matters. People become experts at mixing strategies:

planting near reliable water, moving herds to where grass remains, maintaining social ties across distance so that a drought in one zone can be offset by kin in another.

Now cross the oceans of time to the **Andes**, where altitude itself shapes agriculture's possibilities.

In the highlands and adjacent ecological tiers of western South America, domestication grows from tubers and grains suited to cold nights and steep slopes: **potatoes**, **quinoa**, and other plants that thrive where wheat would struggle. Camelids—**llamas and alpacas**—are domesticated from wild ancestors, becoming pack animals and sources of wool and meat. Timelines vary by species and region, but many key developments unfold across the long span from roughly **8000 to 3000 BCE**, with gradual intensification rather than a single turning point.

Here, "field" can mean terraced hillside. It can mean raised beds designed to manage frost and water. It can mean patchwork cultivation across microclimates: coastal valleys, mid-elevation zones, high puna grasslands. The Andean world teaches a different lesson than the Fertile Crescent: agriculture is not one environment's answer exported to everywhere. It is a family of answers shaped by altitude, water, and the ability to coordinate labor in difficult terrain.

And then there is **Mesoamerica**, where one of the most consequential domestications on Earth begins with a grass that barely resembles its descendant.

Early maize comes from **teosinte**, a wild plant whose tiny, hard kernels do not look like the corn that will later feed empires. The transformation is slow and patient, a chain of selections and replantings that may stretch over millennia. Many researchers discuss early maize domestication beginning perhaps around **7000–4000 BCE**, with intensification and dependence developing later, differing by region and evidence. Alongside maize, crops like **beans** and **squash** become part of a complementary system, each helping the others in soil and diet.

Here the garden plot turning into a field is a domestication of landscape and taste. People learn to prefer certain traits, to save seeds that suit human needs, to return to the same plants not because the wild world is empty, but because planned food can be counted on. And once maize becomes dependable, it becomes portable. It travels. It becomes a base for villages and, eventually, cities.

Across all these regions, the pattern repeats: domestication is not simply about inventing food. It is about managing risk, time, and labor.

Why did humans do it? There is no single motive that fits every place, but the pressures are familiar.

In some regions, climate stability made longer stays feasible, and longer stays made cultivation efficient. In others, climate volatility made cultivation attractive as insurance. Population growth and crowding meant that rich foraging zones could not absorb everyone, pushing communities toward intensifying production. Social life mattered too. Feasting, ritual gatherings, and obligations can create demand for predictable surplus. If your status depends on feeding others, you begin to care deeply about guaranteed food. If your community needs to provision builders, ritual specialists, or warriors, storage and cultivation become tools of organization.

And there is another motivation that is easy to overlook because it is so ordinary: familiarity. People gather plants for generations. They learn their lifecycles. They notice where they grow best. They learn that disturbed soil near a settlement sprouts useful species. They replant.

They protect. Over time, managing plants begins to feel like common sense.

Still, none of these beginnings were inevitable. Farming is costly. It ties you to place, making you vulnerable to drought, flood, pests, and raids. It demands backbreaking labor at specific times of year. It can reduce dietary diversity at first. Many communities likely resisted dependence on cultivation for as long as they could, or used it as a supplement rather than a foundation. Even within regions that adopt agriculture, strategies vary. People mix hunting, fishing, gathering, herding, and farming in different proportions. There is no single ladder of progress here. There are choices. The consequences begin small and then accumulate.

Once crops and herds become central, people store more. Storage makes property more meaningful. Property invites rules. Rules invite authority. Authority invites conflict. Villages grow. Some become permanent. Some become centers that draw others in. And because agriculture produces surplus that can be measured, it becomes a foundation for inequality as well as security. Who controls the storehouse? Who owns the best land? Who claims the water? These questions are not side effects. They are embedded in the new system.

Back at the seed basket, the hand makes its quiet decision and the seeds fall into the chosen pile. The act is humble, almost invisible against the scale of history. But it carries a heavy future. Once you begin selecting life to suit human needs, you are no longer only living within ecosystems. You are shaping them.

7

Taming the Wild

The grinding stone has its own sound, a steady scrape that fills the space between breaths. Grain breaks down under pressure, turning from hard kernels into pale flour that dusts the hands and settles into the creases of skin. The work is rhythmic, almost hypnotic, but it is not gentle. Knees ache. Wrists stiffen. Shoulders burn in a way that hunting rarely demanded, because this labor does not come in bursts. It returns every morning. It returns every evening. It returns because the household must eat, and because a village can only stay a village if someone keeps turning harvest into meals.

Earlier, we discussed how farming began in more than one place for more than one reason, here we'll see what happened when that experiment moved from the edge of life to the center of it. Domestication did not only change landscapes. It changed bodies. It changed time. It changed relationships between men and women, between parents and children, between neighbors, between humans and animals. It made food more predictable in one sense, and it made life more fragile in another.

In the earliest agricultural villages of **Southwest Asia**, beginning after roughly **10,000 BCE** and accelerating through the millennia that follow, the new way of eating begins quietly. People still hunt. They still gather. But their daily calories increasingly come from a narrower menu: cultivated cereals and pulses, stored and cooked into porridge and bread. This shift is visible in teeth and bones across many regions where farming takes hold. Dental decay becomes more common in some populations, because sticky carbohydrates feed the bacteria that damage enamel. Signs of nutritional stress, like enamel defects that mark hard childhoods, can appear alongside the growing stability of settlement. In some places, average stature declines compared to earlier foragers, a reminder that "more food" does not automatically mean "better food," especially when diets become less varied.

The village changes the body not only through diet, but through workload. Foragers worked hard, but their labor was often flexible, adaptive, and mobile. Farming and village life concentrate labor into repetitive tasks and seasonal bottlenecks. Fields must be cleared and tended. Harvest must be timed precisely. Grain must be processed, stored, guarded from moisture, rodents, and thieves. Grinding alone consumes countless hours. When archaeologists find worn grinding stones and heavy querns in early villages, they are not just finding kitchen tools. They are finding a new schedule of life. And domestication is not just plant domestication. Animals step into the human household in ways that transform everything.

In Southwest Asia, sheep and goats are among the earliest domesticated herd animals, with strong evidence for management and selective culling emerging in the early Holocene, broadly in the **9th and 8th millennia BCE**. Cattle follow, and pigs are brought into human systems in different regions and trajectories. Whatever the precise local sequence, the core change is the same: humans stop treating animals only as prey and begin treating them as living capital.

Herding reorganizes movement even for people who are otherwise settling down. Fields anchor a village, but animals still need grazing and water. A herder's seasonal route becomes part of the village's heartbeat, pushing outward into hills and steppe and returning again. Herds bring meat, hides, bone for tools, and manure that can enrich fields. They also bring conflict. A herd is stealable. Grazing rights can be contested. The landscape becomes partitioned not just by where food grows, but by who claims the right to move animals through it.

Then there is milk. It is easy to miss how radical milk is until you see what it offers: calories on the hoof, renewable protein and fat without slaughter. Dairying is not the first thing herders do everywhere, and early humans were mostly lactose intolerant as adults. Yet people learned to work around biology. Fermentation turns milk into yogurt and cheese, reducing lactose and extending shelf life. The evidence for early dairying is not a folk tale. It shows up in chemistry, in the residues preserved in pottery. In parts of Neolithic Europe and Southwest Asia, researchers have identified lipid residues that point to dairy fats in vessels, suggesting that by the time farming villages are established across wide zones, people are already experimenting with milk as a staple, not merely a curiosity.

That matters because it shows domestication as a two-way transformation. Humans shape animals, but animals also shape human lifeways. Over much longer spans, cultural practices like dairying create evolutionary pressure that helps explain why lactase persistence becomes common in some later populations. In the early villages themselves, the more immediate effect is practical: dairying increases the range of foods that can be produced from a herd, making households less dependent on the timing of slaughter and more able to survive lean seasons. But new foods and new routines come with new risks, and some of those risks are carried on hooves and in breath.

When animals live closer to people, parasites and pathogens gain opportunities. Pens near houses attract insects and rodents. Waste concentrates. Water sources become more easily contaminated. Some of the great "crowd diseases" that later sweep through cities require large, dense populations to persist, and they likely do not fully take hold until much later. But the early village still sees a shift in disease ecology. Zoonoses do not arrive as a single plague bell that rings. They arrive as an increased background of infections and exposures, a gradual tightening of the web between species. Brucellosis, for example, is associated with livestock and dairy in later historical contexts, and tuberculosis has deep roots with complex animal-human histories. It is hard to pin every early illness to a specific microbe, but the direction is consistent: domestication brings humans into more frequent contact with animal-borne risks, and sedentism makes it harder to simply walk away from contaminated spaces.

If the village is a machine for producing food, it is also a machine for producing property. Foragers can have possessions, but mobility puts limits on accumulation. A settled household can store grain, keep tools, build heavier structures, and mark space as "ours." Storage pits and granaries are not only practical solutions. They are social thresholds. Once food is stored, questions become unavoidable. Who controls the key? Who decides distribution in a bad year? Who inherits when a household head dies? Who is allowed to marry into the group and gain access to land? Even before formal states, these questions shape power.

You can feel this in architecture. In some early villages, houses become more than shelters; they become statements of belonging and continuity. Floors are renewed. Walls are replastered. In places like **Çatalhöyük** in Anatolia, flourishing later in the Neolithic (roughly **7100–6000 BCE**), households often contain burials beneath floors. Whatever the precise ritual meanings, the message is tangible: the dead are kept close, and the house becomes a lineage anchor. Place becomes identity.

This is where gendered labor often intensifies. It is dangerous to paint a single global picture, because roles vary across cultures and time, and the past does not always mirror later stereotypes. Still, the pressures of village life tend to sort work in ways that leave marks on bodies. Grinding and food processing, childcare, textile production, and many domestic tasks often fall heavily on women in many agrarian societies, while hunting, herding, long-distance exchange, and heavy field labor can be more male-coded in many contexts. The crucial point is not a simplistic division. It is that domestication expands the labor load and makes certain kinds of work relentless, repetitive, and physically taxing. A village does not run on inspiration. It runs on daily effort that rarely leaves monuments.

As diets change and settlement stabilizes, fertility patterns can change too. Mobile foragers often space births because carrying multiple very young children while moving is punishing and risky. In villages, with stored food and more stable shelter, birth intervals can shorten. Earlier weaning is possible when cereal gruels or other soft foods supplement breastfeeding. Grandparents and older siblings can contribute to childcare in a more anchored community. Over time, more surviving children can mean faster population growth, which feeds back into the pressures that make farming seem necessary in the first place.

That growth, however, intensifies vulnerability. A larger village needs more food, which can push fields outward, which can increase labor demands and environmental impacts. Crop failures hit harder when more people depend on the harvest. Malnutrition can appear not because people are starving constantly, but because diets become monotonous and micronutrients become harder to obtain. Iron deficiency and other nutritional stresses can become more common where reliance on grains and limited protein becomes pronounced. The village can be both more secure and more brittle than the older mobile world.

And then there are the children, at the center of all these changes. A village cemetery tells the story in a way no theory can fully soften. In some early settled communities, archaeologists find graves that include infants and young children, sometimes with small objects placed alongside them. A bead necklace. A shell. A piece of worked bone. A token that says this life mattered, that this death is not only private grief but communal memory. The presence of grave goods does not tell us exactly what people believed about an afterlife, but it tells us what they believed about belonging. Even a child who never grew into a laborer, a parent, or an elder is still folded into the social fabric.

Now return to that pottery sherd with invisible evidence baked into it. Somewhere in a village, a pot once held milk or a fermented dairy product, warmed near a hearth, shared among household members. No one knew that thousands of years later, that fat would still cling to the ceramic and speak to scientists. Yet it does. It tells us that domestication was not only about owning animals. It was about learning new ways to extract life from them, new ways to store calories, new ways to keep children fed.

Domestication rewired daily life because it changed the unit of survival. In the old mobile world, the band moved with the seasons, and social networks provided backup across distance. In the village world, the household becomes heavier, anchored in walls and stored food. The household's success depends on fields, herds, and the ability to defend and manage them. The village becomes a place where cooperation is constant and conflict is unavoidable, where property is both security and temptation, where disease is both familiar and newly shaped by proximity.

It is easy, from a modern distance, to treat agriculture as the obvious next step in human progress. But when you watch it unfold at ground level, it looks less like destiny and more like trade-offs. Grain fills bellies but can thin diets. Herds provide wealth but invite theft and disease. Storage buffers famine but fuels inequality. Settlement supports children but increases vulnerability to failure. The village is not simply better than the camp. It is different, with consequences that compound.

The grinding stone keeps scraping. The work keeps returning. Outside, animals bleat from pens or from the edge of pasture. Somewhere a pot simmers. Somewhere a child coughs and is soothed. Somewhere, under a floor or in a cemetery, a small grave is closed, and the living step back into their routines, carrying grief alongside obligation.

8

From Hamlets to Megasites

In the early morning, before the heat settles in, the settlement is already awake. Smoke rises in thin columns from hearths that have not been allowed to die. Footsteps thud along packed paths between houses. Somewhere a dog barks and a child answers it, half-laughing, half-scolding. The air carries the smell of damp clay, ash, and grain dust. From the edge of the village you can see storage pits marked by low mounds and patches of trampled ground where people have gathered again and again—loading, unloading, arguing, counting.

Then you notice something that wasn't there in the smaller hamlets. Some houses are bigger. Not just by a little. Bigger enough to change how you move through a doorway. Bigger enough to hold more people, more goods, more tools, more stored food. Bigger enough to make you wonder, without anyone saying it out loud, who is doing better than whom—and why.

For most of human history, the limits of settlement kept social problems within a manageable range. In a small camp or a scattered hamlet, conflict can be defused by distance. People can split and move. Authority can be informal. If someone hoards too much, everyone knows it; if someone becomes dangerous, the group can pressure them, abandon them, or leave.

But in the Neolithic world, those escape valves begin to narrow. Once people store food, build heavier houses, bury their dead in or near homes, and invest in fields and herds, moving away becomes costly. And once communities grow beyond a certain size, everyone cannot know everyone. Strangers become neighbors. Neighbors become problems. Problems demand systems.

This is where villages begin to grow into something larger—dense settlements that can hold hundreds or thousands of people, sometimes in astonishing concentrations. The dates and examples differ by region, but the basic shift becomes visible in multiple places between roughly **7000 and 4000 BCE**: settlement size increases, permanence deepens, and the social world becomes more stratified, more organized, and more tense.

To see why, start with storage.

In a hamlet, storage can be household-scale: baskets, jars, pits. In a larger settlement, storage becomes politics. Grain does not simply sit in the ground; it sits under claim. Someone dug the pit. Someone guarded it. Someone decides what happens when a harvest fails, when a neighbor asks for a loan, when a work crew must be fed, when a feast must be staged. The more food can be stored, the more power can be stored with it.

Now add property. Fields are cleared and maintained; herds are managed; tools accumulate. Households begin to look less equal because their assets diverge. Some have better land, more animals, stronger kin connections, better access to trade routes, or simply better luck. Over generations, those differences harden. Inequality becomes visible, not in a single tyrant's crown, but in subtle signals: house size, quality of construction, access to rare materials, the presence of prestige goods, the ability to host feasts, the control of storage.

The archaeological record often captures this in architecture. House-size differences are one of the simplest inequality signals because they are literally built into the settlement's layout. A larger house can mean many things—extended family structure, specialized production, communal functions—but persistent patterns of size and richness can also suggest that some households command more labor and resources than others. The village stops being a cluster of roughly similar units and becomes a landscape of distinction.

Distinction creates tension, and tension creates the need for coordination and control.

In a settlement of thousands, basic logistics become a daily challenge. Water must be managed. Waste must be dealt with. Fires must be controlled, or they will race through closely packed structures. Food must be produced beyond immediate needs, stored safely, redistributed in predictable ways. Disputes must be settled, or feuds will spiral. People must be brought together for shared work—building, harvesting, defense—without constant negotiation as if every task were voluntary.

That is a lot to ask of informal persuasion alone. So the settlement begins to grow institutions—sometimes visible, sometimes not. Some of those institutions are religious. Ritual authority often becomes more important as communities scale, because rituals create shared time and shared identity. In smaller groups, belonging is obvious; in larger ones, it must be performed and renewed. A ritual platform, a shrine space, a communal structure used for feasting or ceremonies—these are not just spiritual centers. They are social technologies. They gather people, synchronize emotion, reinforce norms, and legitimize leadership roles. A person who can speak for the gods, ancestors, or cosmic order gains leverage in disputes that would otherwise be settled by brute force or endless argument.

Ritual also provides a language for inequality. If one household is wealthier, it can frame that wealth as sacred responsibility: donors, patrons, guardians. It can sponsor ceremonies that make hierarchy feel like tradition rather than theft. This is one way societies often solve the problem of unequal resources without constant violence: by making the unequal order seem meaningful and stable.

But violence does not disappear. If anything, the evidence for conflict often becomes sharper as settlement size increases and the cost of leaving rises.

Picture a palisade: thick wooden posts sunk into the ground, packed close, forming a barrier that says the outside is dangerous and the inside is defended. Palisades require labor. They require planning. They imply a threat worth the cost. In different regions and periods, archaeologists have found signs of defensive works and violent trauma—skulls with fractures, embedded projectile points, burned structures, abandoned layers that suggest sudden disruption. Not every large settlement is a fortress, and not every injury is war. But the pattern is hard to ignore: as resources concentrate, so do incentives to seize them.

A megasite—an exceptionally large settlement—magnifies all these dynamics.

Some of the most striking examples appear in Neolithic and Chalcolithic contexts, including very large settlements in parts of eastern Europe (often associated with the Cucuteni–Trypillia tradition, later than the earliest Southwest Asian villages), and dense settlement forms elsewhere. The specifics vary, but the concept is consistent: at a certain scale, a settlement becomes an organism with internal organs—specialized zones, production areas, storage systems, ritual spaces, and, often, social hierarchies that are not always obvious from a single "palace" or royal tomb.

This matters because it challenges a simplistic story: "villages become cities when kings appear." Sometimes the settlement grows first, driven by ecology, technology, and social networks, and only later do clearly centralized states emerge. Megasites show that large-scale living can exist in forms that are complex and sometimes surprisingly non-monarchical, yet still require coordination and still generate inequality pressures.

You can feel those pressures in the everyday scene. A household brings baskets of grain to a storage area. Someone measures. Someone records in memory or token. A dispute breaks out: the measure is unfair, the claim is false, the labor contribution was greater than recognized. A ritual leader may intervene, invoking norms that are framed as sacred. An elder council may decide. Or a stronger household may impose its will. However it happens, the settlement needs closure. Without closure, it fractures.

At the same time, the settlement is building belief. People living closely together share more than walls. They share anxieties: about harvest failure, sickness, fire, raids, social betrayal. Belief systems often thicken under such conditions because they offer explanations and controls where human control is partial. Ritual can promise protection. Ancestors can be invoked to justify land claims. Sacred spaces can mediate conflict. The village becomes not only an economic unit but a moral universe.

What are the consequences when hamlets scale into megasites?

In the short term, bigger settlements can produce stability and surplus. They can support specialists—potters, weavers, builders, ritual experts. They can concentrate knowledge and innovation. They can organize large projects: irrigation ditches, storage complexes, communal buildings. They can attract trade, drawing in materials and ideas that a small hamlet would never see.

But they also produce fragility. Disease spreads faster in dense populations. Fire spreads faster. Conflict becomes costlier. Inequality becomes harder to ignore and harder to reverse. The settlement must constantly manage internal tensions to prevent splintering or collapse.

In the long term, megasites and large villages become the proving ground for something even bigger: the emergence of states. Not because every megasite becomes a state, but because the problems they face—coordination, coercion, legitimacy, property enforcement—are precisely the problems states claim to solve. The tools that appear here—formal storage systems, standardized measures, ritual authority, defensive organization—are the early infrastructure of later political power.

Return to the morning village. People move along the paths. Smoke rises. Grain dust clings to skin. In one house, there is enough stored food to host a feast; in another, there is barely enough to make it to next season. Near the edge, workers repair a palisade post, hammering it deeper into the earth. On a raised platform, someone arranges offerings, preparing for a ceremony that will gather the settlement into one body—at least for a day. The settlement is no longer simply a place to live. It is a machine that produces order, and a machine that produces tension.

9

Tools That Built Worlds

The loom weights are cool in the hand—small lumps of fired clay, each pierced and smoothed by use. They hang in rows, tugging threads taut, turning a loose bundle of fiber into something ordered. The rhythm in the room is soft but constant: the tap of the weft, the pull, the tightening, the small creak of wood. Outside, someone drags a heavy tool through soil still damp from rain. The earth opens in a clean line, darker underneath than on the surface. In that furrow, the future sits like a promise and a threat at the same time.

When people talk about the Neolithic, they often talk as if farming alone did the work of transforming the world. But farming is only one part of the engine. Villages do not scale into large settlements—and large settlements do not hold together—without a web of ordinary technologies that make life more predictable, more productive, and more coordinated. These inventions rarely look dramatic in a museum case. A lump of clay. A sharpened stone. A bit of copper hammered thin. A boat scraped and sealed. Yet each one solves a problem that emerges the moment humans stop moving constantly and start living among stored food, property, and strangers.

The first of these technologies is the one you can hold in your palm: pottery. A clay pot is more than a container. It is a time machine. It lets you boil grains and legumes into food that can be digested more easily. It lets you store water safely and carry it farther. It lets you keep oils, fats, and fermented products. It turns seasonal abundance into year-round security. When archaeologists find pottery styles spreading through regions, they are often seeing not merely "art" but a practical response to settled life: the need to store, cook, share, and trade.

And pottery is also information. A pot's shape and decoration can mark who made it, where it belongs, what group it signals. In a world where villages multiply and trade networks thicken, style becomes identity. A vessel sitting on a hearth can quietly announce "us" and "not us" without a word.

Weaving does something similar, and often more. Cloth is easy to underestimate because it disappears. But in the Neolithic, textiles can be as transformative as stone blades. Fiber becomes rope, which becomes binding, which becomes nets, which becomes the ability to catch fish more efficiently and transport goods more safely. Rope makes lifting and hauling possible. It turns heavy objects—timbers, stones, boats—into feasible projects for coordinated labor. Cloth becomes clothing, and clothing is survival at the margins of cold and wet. Cloth becomes sacks for grain. Cloth becomes trade goods. Cloth becomes a form of wealth that can be carried.

Loom weights, spindle whorls, and impressions in clay hint at workshops and household production. Weaving also reshapes labor patterns. It demands long hours and skill, and it often becomes deeply gendered in many agrarian societies, though the exact divisions vary. The point is not only who weaves. It is that weaving ties people to a rhythm of repetitive work that fits sedentary life and produces outputs that can be stored and exchanged. A community with surplus cloth can trade for things it cannot produce locally. Technology, in this sense, extends geography.

Now step outside, to the field and the line in the soil. The plow mark is one of the most consequential scars humans ever made. Before plows, fields can be worked with digging sticks and hoes. That is effective but labor-intensive. A plow—especially when pulled by animals—changes the scale of cultivation. It breaks soil faster, opens larger fields, and makes expansion possible in a way that reshapes landscapes and social relations. It is not only a tool. It is an amplifier. And like all amplifiers, it does not distribute its benefits evenly.

To use a plow efficiently, you often need draft animals, which means herds and the wealth and land access that support them. Plow agriculture can therefore deepen inequality, because households that control animals and land can produce more surplus, acquire more property, and command more labor. The technology that increases productivity can also increase hierarchy.

The wheel belongs in the same family of quiet revolutions. A wheel seems obvious now, but it is not an inevitable thought. It requires a certain way of imagining rotation and load. Once it exists, it reshapes movement of goods. Carts can move harvests, building materials, and trade items more efficiently than human backs alone. Roads become worth maintaining. Villages become nodes rather than isolated dots. The wheel does not just speed travel; it changes what kinds of economies can exist. Larger settlements can be supplied more regularly. Surplus can be moved to markets or stored centrally. Power can reach farther.

And movement is not only over land. If the wheel changes land logistics, boats change the map itself. Rivers and coasts become highways. A canoe is one of the most elegant tools ever designed: hollowed wood or lashed planks that turn water from barrier to corridor. In many regions, long before formal states exist, people use boats to move goods, people, and ideas along river systems and across short sea routes. In island worlds and coastal zones, seafaring becomes a way of life. Even small boats expand the radius of connection.

You can picture a canoe gliding along a river at dawn. Mist rises off the water. The paddles make a soft, rhythmic slap. In the bottom of the craft are baskets, jars, bundles of fiber, perhaps stone blades or shells traded from another shore. The people in the canoe are not conquering the world. They are linking it. Their route ties one village to another, one resource zone to another, one kin network to another. In a world of growing settlements, these watery corridors help stabilize supply and spread innovations.

Then comes metal—not as an instant replacement for stone, but as an experiment that begins small and grows.

In the late Neolithic and early Chalcolithic periods in some regions, people begin working native copper and other accessible metals. At first, metal is often hammered rather than cast—shaped cold, then annealed, then shaped again. It can be used for ornaments, small tools, and prestige goods before it becomes the foundation of weapon systems and state economies. The beginnings of metallurgy matter because they reveal a new relationship with materials: not only shaping stone that already exists in usable form, but transforming matter through heat and chemistry.

Metalworking also intensifies trade, because metals are unevenly distributed. Copper, tin, and later alloys pull communities into longer-distance exchanges. A settlement near a metal source gains leverage. A settlement far from it must negotiate access. Metallurgy becomes a driver of interregional connection long before empires enforce routes.

All of these technologies—pots, looms, plows, wheels, boats, metal—do something similar at a deeper level. They make societies scalable by making life predictable.

Predictability, however, requires timekeeping. You cannot manage planting and harvest well without paying attention to seasons. You cannot coordinate communal labor without agreed schedules. You cannot host rituals that bind a community without shared calendars. Neolithic societies develop ways of tracking time that do not require writing: observing solstices, lunar cycles, star risings, seasonal winds, animal migrations. Some built spaces that may align with celestial events, though interpretations vary and scholars debate which alignments are intentional and how they were used. But the broader truth is uncontroversial: as people settle and invest in fields and storage, time becomes a resource that must be measured, not merely felt.

A calendar is also power. The person or institution that declares when a festival occurs, when planting begins, when communal labor is required, can shape the rhythm of the entire settlement. Timekeeping can be a religious function, an administrative function, or both. It is another way that technology and authority braid together.

What does this look like on the ground?

It looks like a household where woven sacks hold grain safe from moisture. It looks like pottery jars lined along a wall, each one a reserve against hunger. It looks like a plow team turning a field that would have taken many more hands to dig by stick. It looks like a canoe arriving at a riverside landing with goods that were impossible to move cheaply by land. It looks like a small piece of copper flashed bright in firelight, worn as status, not because it feeds anyone, but because it says something about connection and access. It looks like people gathering at a certain moon phase because tradition says this is when the community acts together.

In the short term, these technologies raise carrying capacity. They help villages grow. They allow more specialization. They make longer-distance exchange easier. They give elites more tools for organizing and extracting, but they also give ordinary households more stability and capacity to survive bad seasons.

In the long term, they prepare the world for the next leap in complexity. Once you can store reliably, move goods efficiently, coordinate labor through shared time, and connect settlements through corridors of trade, you have the infrastructure for something that begins to appear in multiple regions: large-scale exchange systems that feel almost state-like even before states. You have the conditions for bureaucracies and writing to become useful, not as mysteries, but as practical solutions.

Return to the loom weights and the furrow in the soil. One is small and steady, the other is a line cut into earth. Neither looks like the birth of civilization. Yet both are exactly that kind of event: a tool that makes a larger world possible. Threads become cloth. Furrows become harvests. Harvests become surplus. Surplus becomes obligation. Obligation becomes authority.

10

First Web of Trade

The blade is too sharp to be ordinary. Even in a world full of stone, this one catches the eye. It is black and glossy, with an edge so clean it looks like it could cut light. Someone turns it in their hand and watches the surface flicker. They know what it is—not just a tool, but a material with a story. Obsidian does not come from anywhere near this village. There are no volcanic flows on these plains, no glassy outcrops in the nearby hills. Yet here it is, lying in a house floor's dust, as if it belongs. It does belong. That is the unsettling part.

Long before kings stamp coins or scribes record tariffs, long before armies guard roads, humans build networks that move things farther than a person can easily walk in a week. These networks are not always "trade" in the modern sense. They include barter, gift exchange, ritual offerings, bridewealth, alliances sealed with objects, and long chains of hand-to-hand movement where no single person travels the full distance. But the result is the same: a wider world comes into being—quietly, cumulatively—until communities begin to depend on strangers they may never meet. That dependence is one of the roots of states.

In the Neolithic and early settled eras, exchange begins with necessity. The village world is productive, but it is not self-sufficient. Some places have good soil but lack stone suitable for tools. Some have clay but lack salt. Some have grain but lack timber. Some have animals but need certain minerals or pigments. Even before metals matter in bulk, high-quality stone matters, and obsidian matters most of all. It fractures into razor edges. It is prized for blades and cutting tools. And because obsidian sources are geographically limited—tied to volcanic regions—its presence far away becomes a map of connection.

Archaeologists can often trace obsidian to specific source areas using geochemical signatures, which is one reason it plays such a starring role in this story. When an obsidian blade shows up hundreds of kilometers from the nearest volcanic source, it is not a mystery artifact. It is proof that people moved or traded across long distances. It is proof that routes existed. It is proof that trust—however fragile—stretched beyond the horizon.

Now picture the same logic with shells. A shell bead found far inland carries the sea like a whisper. It tells you someone traveled to a coast, or someone met someone who did, or someone traded with someone who traded with someone who did. Shells are light, durable, and easily turned into ornament. They become ideal vehicles for meaning. In a world where many groups are newly sedentary—where fields, storage, and herds tie people to place—ornament becomes a way to carry social connection when bodies do not move as freely. A strand of beads can signal affiliation, marriage ties, alliance obligations. It can also signal status, because not everyone has equal access to distant luxuries.

And then there is amber: fossilized resin, golden in sunlight, warm to the touch, rare in many regions. Amber routes—later famous in European prehistory—show how certain materials become magnetic, pulling communities into networks that can span enormous distances for their time. The specific intensities and dates of "amber routes" vary, and many of the most documented long-distance amber movements flourish later, but the principle belongs here: some materials become prestige goods because they are scarce, beautiful, and portable. Prestige goods are not frivolous. They are social tools.

To understand why, think about what exchange is doing in a world before states. It is solving problems that the village cannot solve alone. If you have surplus grain but lack good stone, exchange converts one advantage into another. If you live near a salt source, salt becomes leverage. If you have skilled potters or weavers, their outputs can travel and bring back rare materials. Exchange also spreads ideas. A new tool form appears far from its origin. A pottery style shifts. A weaving technique spreads. A ritual object becomes fashionable. Over generations, these flows create shared cultural zones, even without political unity.

But exchange also creates vulnerability. If a community depends on certain imported materials—obsidian for cutting, salt for preservation, timber for building—then disruption along routes becomes a crisis. The more interconnected the world becomes, the more a problem in one place can echo in another.

Networks widen opportunity and widen risk. This is where "trade hubs" begin to matter.

Even without formal cities, certain places function as magnets: river crossings, lake shores, coastal landings, mountain passes, oases, and the edges of ecological zones where different resources meet. People gather there seasonally or regularly. Goods accumulate. Information spreads. Marriage arrangements are negotiated. Disputes are mediated. Feasts reinforce alliances. These hubs are not always permanent settlements. Sometimes they are recurring meeting places—ritual and commercial at once—where the social world renews itself.

Imagine a hub at a river junction. Canoes arrive from upstream and downstream. People carry baskets, hides, pottery, bundles of fiber, and small precious items wrapped in cloth. There is tension in the air because strangers are present, and strangers are always a risk. But there is also necessity. The village needs what the river brings. The river brings not only goods, but news: a drought upriver, a new group moving in, a conflict near the pass, a rumor of rich hunting grounds. In such a place, exchange is inseparable from diplomacy. This is where kinship becomes infrastructure.

Marriage alliances are among the most powerful ways humans stabilize networks. When you marry into another group, you turn potential enemies into relatives. You create obligations that can outlast a bad season. You create routes that are not just paths on the ground but paths through people: places where you will be received, fed, and protected because your sister's children live there, because your lineage is tied to theirs. In many small-scale societies, long-distance connections are maintained less by merchants as a separate class and more by kin relations that make travel safe.

Objects often travel along these kin routes. Bridewealth can move wealth across groups. Gifts can seal alliances. Prestige goods can mark the seriousness of a bond. A shell bead far inland may be the residue of marriage politics, not a marketplace transaction. Now add conflict and the picture sharpens.

As villages grow and store more, they become tempting targets. Stored grain is wealth that cannot run away. Herds can be stolen. Fields can be seized. Routes can be controlled. Exchange networks create incentives for protection—sometimes through alliances, sometimes through violence. A group that sits astride a pass or controls a river landing can extract tolls in goods or labor. A group that monopolizes access to obsidian or salt can convert geography into power. Even before formal states, you can see the outlines of what states will later claim to do: secure routes, enforce agreements, punish theft, adjudicate disputes.

But in this era, enforcement is often personal and negotiated. It depends on reputation, kin ties, reciprocal obligations, and the threat of retaliation. That makes it fragile. A broken agreement can cascade into raiding. A theft can become a feud. A feud can break a network.

This fragility is exactly why larger political structures become attractive later. States do not arise only from conquest. They also arise from the demand for predictable order in an increasingly connected world.

To feel how this works, picture a traveler's pack. It is not a modern backpack. It is a bundle wrapped in woven cloth or hide, tied with cord, balanced on the back or slung over the shoulder. Inside are objects chosen with care because weight matters: a few obsidian blades, perhaps, or a core that can be knapped into blades later; a small pouch of beads; a piece of pigment; maybe a fine textile; perhaps salt wrapped to keep it dry. The traveler also carries something less visible: relationships. Names of people in the next settlement who owe favors. Knowledge of which paths are safe. Stories of recent disputes. The traveler is not a lone hero. They are a moving node in a network, and their safety depends on the network holding.

In the short term, exchange before states accelerates innovation and specialization. It allows settlements to thrive in places where they lack key resources. It creates cultural zones wider than any single community. It spreads tool forms, pottery styles, and ritual practices. It also creates new social differences as some households or lineages gain better access to prestige goods and far-flung connections.

In the long term, it lays down the arteries that later states will inherit and attempt to control. Routes become predictable. Hubs grow. Certain locations become strategic. Institutions that can offer protection, standardize measures, and enforce agreements gain an advantage. The desire to secure exchange becomes one of the pressures that pushes societies toward more formal authority.

Return to the obsidian blade, still gleaming in a village far from any volcano. Its edge is practical, but its journey is the real story. It has passed through hands that never met each other, across landscapes that changed with season and weather, along routes held together by trust and risk. It proves that the world is already connected—before writing, before kings, before borders.

Part III

Rivers, Cities, and States (c. 3500–1200 BCE)

11

When Writing Took Over

The tablet is still damp. Clay holds the cold of the storeroom, and it stains the lines of the scribe's palm the way river mud stains everything in this place. Outside, the sun is already high, bleaching the walls and turning the canal into a strip of hard light. Inside, the air smells of grain dust and sour beer. A foreman stands by the doorway with a handful of names and a problem. A work crew has finished dredging a clogged channel. They want their rations. They want them now, before the heat turns bad-tempered and the day slips into exhaustion. The scribe does not argue. He does not perform. He sets the clay across his knee and begins. Wedge marks. Lines. A sign for barley. Another for beer. A sign that indicates measure rather than poetry. It is a ration list, and it has the quiet force of a boundary stone. The tablet says what is owed. It says who counts. It says who has the authority to turn labor into food and food into obedience.

In a small village, a promise can live in the air between two people. In a city, a promise must be made into an object. That is the heart of Mesopotamia's transformation. Cities, accounting, and kingship do not arrive as separate inventions that politely take turns. They grow together, each making the others more necessary. Once you build a dense settlement on a floodplain, you create problems that only record-keeping can solve. Once you have record-keeping, you can coordinate labor at a scale that invites monumental building and war. Once war and monumentality become regular, rulers emerge who claim the right to command. And once rulers command, they need bureaucracy to keep the machine from shaking itself apart. This is how the world tips from village-scale life into something new.

The land between the **Tigris and Euphrates** is often described as a cradle, but the metaphor can mislead. Cradles suggest softness. Mesopotamia's plain is productive and unforgiving at the same time. Rain is unreliable, especially in the south. The sun is constant. Water must be managed, coaxed through canals, kept from turning fields into salt. When irrigation works, the alluvium can produce dense harvests of barley and dates. When it fails, hunger arrives quickly, because a large population cannot simply scatter back into the countryside without leaving behind fields, storage pits, houses, and the dead. By **c. 3500 BCE**, communities in the south were already living with this bargain. Then, in the late fourth millennium BCE, one place in particular begins to expand in ways that are hard to ignore: **Uruk**.

Archaeologists do not "see" population directly, but they see what population leaves behind: expanding built-up areas, intensified production, monumental architecture, deep layers of occupation. At Uruk, between roughly **c. 4000 and 3100 BCE**, the scale of settlement appears to leap. Temples and public buildings rise. Specialized crafts intensify. Administrative tools multiply. The city becomes more than a place where people live; it becomes a system that must be run.

Running a system requires measurement. Grain must be counted. Beer must be allocated. Labor must be scheduled. Herds must be tracked. Offerings must be recorded. Disputes must be resolved. And in a city, the "memory" of the community can no longer live solely in elders' recollections and face-to-face reputation. Too many strangers. Too many transactions. Too much at stake. This is where writing enters the world, not with a burst of literature but with the steady logic of administration.

By **c. 3200–3000 BCE**, the earliest known Mesopotamian writing appears in the form often called **proto-cuneiform**: signs impressed or drawn on clay, largely used for lists, tallies, and allocations. The medium is not accidental. Clay is everywhere in the river plain. Reeds are everywhere along the marshes and canal edges. A stylus is cheap. A tablet is cheap. In a world where information suddenly matters as much as grain, low-cost record-keeping is a revolution.

What those early tablets do is simple and enormous: they make obligations portable and persistent. A spoken promise fades. A tablet remains. A witness can die or lie. A sealed record can travel. A list can be audited. A ration tablet turns a messy social world into categories an institution can manage.

And the institutions that benefit most are the ones already positioned to concentrate resources: temples and, increasingly, palaces. It is tempting to picture the temple only as a religious building. In early Mesopotamia, temple complexes are also economic and administrative centers. They hold land. They store grain. They organize labor. They sponsor craft production. They anchor calendars of festivals and obligations. They redistribute rations. Their legitimacy is religious, but their power is practical. If a temple controls the storerooms, it can feed workers on a building project, provision a canal dredging crew, and stabilize a population in a lean season. It can also demand labor and extract surplus. The moral language of offering and sacred duty can soften the edge of coercion, but it does not remove it. The temple economy leaves behind a paper trail made of clay. Ration lists like the one drying in the storeroom shade are not rare anomalies. They are the nervous system of the early city: information that allows a concentrated population to function.

As writing evolves into full **cuneiform**, it expands beyond counting. Signs become more standardized. Scribes become a trained class, learning not only how to mark quantities but how to categorize people and goods, how to record names, how to store claims. Scribes, in a sense, become the city's internal memory. They do not rule like kings. But they make ruling possible.

Meanwhile, the city's dependence on distant resources pushes it outward into exchange networks that predate empires and help create them. Southern Mesopotamia is rich in grain and mud, but it lacks many materials needed for building and prestige: timber, stone, and key metals. These must be obtained through trade or controlled access. Routes run north and west toward **Anatolia** and the **Levant**, east toward the **Zagros** and Iranian plateau, and south down the **Persian Gulf**. Later Mesopotamian texts remember maritime nodes like **Dilmun** (often associated with Bahrain) and speak of **Meluhha**, usually linked by many scholars to the **Indus** world. The volume and mechanics of these connections varied across centuries, and the exact identification of far places can be debated, but the broad web is real: Mesopotamia's cities are networked, because the plain forces them to be.

You can feel that network in the scene of a caravan. A line of donkeys moves along a dusty track, packs creaking, hooves tapping a rhythm into hard ground. The merchants do not travel empty-handed. They carry textiles, oil, finished goods, perhaps grain in some contexts, and they return with what the southern plain cannot produce: metals, timber, stone, exotic shells, semi-precious materials. They stop at known watering points and settlements where they have contacts, obligations, kin ties, or agreements enforced by local authorities. At night, they sleep near their animals, because a donkey is not just transport. It is capital.

Caravans and boats are not only economic actors. They are political. Whoever controls chokepoints can extract tolls. Whoever can protect routes can demand loyalty. Whoever can standardize measures can become indispensable. Long-distance exchange creates wealth, but it also creates the pressure for reliable enforcement. A world of trade without trusted adjudication is a world of feuds. This is one reason kingship grows in tandem with administration.

In the centuries after Uruk's growth, Mesopotamia becomes a landscape of competing cities, often called the **Early Dynastic** period (roughly **c. 2900–2350 BCE**, with fuzzy edges depending on region and chronology). Later king lists and inscriptions name cities like **Ur, Uruk, Lagash, Kish**, each with its own patron deities and ambitions. These sources are political documents, not neutral histories, but they reflect a basic reality: multiple urban centers compete over land, water, and status.

Competition intensifies the need for leadership that can mobilize labor and violence. Walls must be built. Canals must be maintained and defended. Work crews must be fed. Soldiers must be provisioned. Disputes must be settled in ways that keep the city from tearing itself apart. In such a world, kingship is not merely a personal ambition. It is a social role that emerges where coordination and coercion become routine. And once kingship exists, it begins to reach for scale.

By the late third millennium BCE, tradition places a dramatic consolidation under **Sargon of Akkad**, usually dated to the start of his reign around **c. 2334 BCE**. Later texts tell stories that are part legend and part political messaging, and the exact contours of Akkadian control likely shifted over time. But the larger development is widely accepted: rule is claimed across multiple cities and regions, not only within a single city-state and its fields. A new political idea becomes practical: empire.

Empire promises solutions. It claims it can secure routes, suppress rivals, standardize measures, and impose order. It also introduces costs: tribute, conscription, resentment from cities that remember older autonomy. Empires depend on logistics, and in Mesopotamia logistics means grain, canals, and records. To provision garrisons and officials across a wide territory, you need administration that can travel: scribes, seals, standardized accounting, enforceable obligations. So the clay archive grows.

Then, as often happens in complex systems, strain accumulates. By around **c. 2154 BCE**, the Akkadian order appears to fragment. Later sources speak of chaos and invasions; modern explanations also consider internal pressures and environmental stress, but the exact mix is debated. What is not debated is the pattern: when a system is stretched across corridors and cities, disruption spreads faster. A drought is not only a local problem. A breakdown in trade is not only economic. A political crisis in one node can ripple through the entire network.

Out of this turbulence emerges another attempt at engineered stability: **Ur III**, often dated **c. 2112–2004 BCE**. Ur III is famous because of the sheer volume of its administrative texts. Labor assignments, rations, audits, deliveries, standardized procedures. If Uruk shows writing being born for accounting, Ur III shows accounting becoming a governing art. The state reaches deeper into daily life, not only to extract but to manage.

For some, this management can feel like security: rations arrive, order holds, routes stabilize. For others, it feels like a tightening net: more categories, more obligations, fewer escape routes. This is one of the enduring truths of administration. It can reduce chaos. It can also reduce freedom. As administration deepens, so does the world of debt.

Once grain and silver-like units of value can be measured, stored, and recorded, lending becomes more enforceable. A bad harvest does not erase a loan. A tablet can carry a claim across time. Debt can pull families into dependence, forcing the sale of land use rights, labor obligations, or household members' service. The details vary across periods, and our evidence is uneven, but the moral shape is consistent: the same record-keeping that makes cities function can also make hardship permanent. This is where law enters the stage not only as custom but as a public claim of legitimacy.

By the early second millennium BCE, political power shifts and recombines across Mesopotamia, including under rulers of Babylon such as **Hammurabi**, often dated **r. c. 1792–1750 BCE**. Hammurabi's law collection, famously inscribed on stone in later copies, is often treated like a modern legal code. It is better understood as a statement of kingship: a performance of order.

The laws address wages, theft, contracts, family disputes, and violence, among many topics. They lay out penalties that differ by social status, reflecting a hierarchical society rather than an egalitarian ideal. They also reveal what kinds of conflicts were common enough to require public articulation: property disputes, debt entanglements, questions of responsibility when things go wrong. You can hear the world behind the clauses: a crowded society where people do business with strangers and need someone to decide whose claim counts.

In a court scene, the drama is not always a battle. Sometimes it is a dispute over barley and repayment, a contract questioned, a boundary argued, a complaint that someone abused power. The judge's decision matters because it transforms a fragile social peace into something that can hold, at least until the next dispute. The state presents itself as the arbiter not because it is always fair, but because without arbitration, the city risks fracture.

That is the co-evolution in full view. Cities create complexity. Complexity demands records. Records empower institutions. Institutions empower rulers. Rulers claim legitimacy through temples, victories, and law. Law stabilizes some conflicts and formalizes inequalities. Trade ties the system to distant regions and makes control of routes politically valuable. Empire attempts to solve rivalry by scaling up coercion and administration. Collapse reminds everyone that systems are fragile. Rebuilding intensifies bureaucracy. The archive grows thicker. The city becomes not just buildings, but paperwork.

Return to the ration tablet drying in the shade. By itself, it is small. You could fit it in a hand. Yet it contains a transformation that will echo across millennia. It turns labor into quantity. It turns food into obligation. It turns a human relationship into an auditable record. It allows power to outlast the moment, to travel beyond the presence of any single person.

Somewhere beyond the canal, a merchant caravan is already moving, dust rising behind the donkeys. Somewhere else, a judge is listening to a complaint and weighing a claim in a world where debts can be recorded and enforced. Somewhere in a temple, offerings are counted and redistributed, and the gods' favor is invoked to justify the flow.

This is Mesopotamia's gift and warning: once humans learn to store not only grain but information, societies can grow to astonishing scale. They can also become bound to systems that are hard to escape.

12

Throne of the Nile

The words are cut deep enough to catch the light. On a limestone wall inside a tomb, the hieroglyphs still hold their crisp edges where the chisel bit clean. A man is shown seated before an offering table piled with bread, beer, and cuts of meat that look too perfect to be ordinary food. Beneath the image runs a formula that repeats across centuries of Egyptian stone: an invocation for offerings, a request that the dead be sustained, a claim that this life mattered and should continue in another form.

Outside the tomb, the desert is silent and hot, a place where nothing decays quickly because almost nothing lives. But beyond the desert's edge the land abruptly changes. A narrow ribbon of green follows the Nile, and in that ribbon the world is loud: water birds, reeds, cattle lowing, people calling across fields. Egypt is built on that sharp contrast. Stone and silt. Death and harvest. A country that can preserve a name for millennia because it sits beside a river that arrives, year after year, with predictable renewal.

If Mesopotamia's cities were forced into constant improvisation by rivers that could be violent and irregular, Egypt's Nile is a different kind of teacher. The Nile's annual inundation, broadly predictable in its season even if not identical in its height, creates a rhythm that can be planned around. Floodwaters spread silt, fields drink, and when the water recedes the land is ready to be planted. This regularity does not eliminate risk. A low flood can mean hunger. A high flood can destroy. But it does something vital for the rise of a durable state: it makes coordination worth the effort, because the payoff returns reliably.

That reliability helps explain why Egypt becomes one of the ancient world's most continuous political traditions, and why it expresses power in stone on a scale that still feels impossible when you stand beneath it.

The story begins with unification, the idea that the Nile valley and delta could be ruled as a single realm. Around **3100 BCE**, Egypt's early dynastic period takes shape, traditionally associated with kings like **Narmer**, whose name appears on artifacts that later ages treat as symbols of consolidation. The details of how unification happened remain debated, and it was likely a process rather than a single event. But the outcome matters. By the early third millennium BCE, Egypt is increasingly governed as a corridor-state: long, narrow, tied together by the river itself.

That geography creates a particular kind of power. Egypt is not a patchwork of city-states like southern Mesopotamia. It is a threaded landscape where the river functions like an artery, linking communities that might otherwise be isolated. A boat can carry grain, stone, officials, and orders. The state can move in ways a purely land-based system struggles to match.

Then, in the **Old Kingdom** (commonly dated **c. 2686–2181 BCE**), the state's ambition takes architectural form. This is the age of pyramids, and pyramids are more than tombs. They are an argument. They argue that the king is not merely a ruler but a sacred pivot, the guarantor of cosmic order. Egyptian kingship is framed through the concept often translated as **ma'at**: balance, justice, proper order, the world held in alignment against chaos. The king is expected to maintain that order through ritual, administration, and authority. In return, the king's power is treated as legitimate and even necessary, woven into the very logic of the universe.

You can see how that becomes practical. If the king is divine or divinely sanctioned, then mobilizing tens of thousands of labor days is not just a political demand. It becomes a sacred duty. Building a pyramid is not only building a grave. It is building the visible proof that order exists and that the state can summon it. To understand how this works, it helps to step away from the pyramid's shining ideal and walk into the dust and noise of the worker village.

Near the Giza plateau, where the pyramids of the Fourth Dynasty rise, archaeology has revealed the remains of labor camps and planned settlements that housed and fed large workforces. The image of pyramid building as a project driven only by enslaved misery is too simple. The workforce likely included a mix of laborers, skilled specialists, and rotating crews drawn through obligation and seasonal availability, especially when the flood season limited agricultural work. Feeding them required bread, beer, meat, and constant logistics. The state had to collect surplus, transport it, distribute it, and record it. Monumentality demanded bureaucracy.

In the worker village, life is not a single triumphant moment. It is sore backs, ration disputes, heat, dust, injuries, and the steady pressure of schedules. It is also community: shared meals, shared burdens, specialized skills passed from hand to hand. The great stone silhouette on the horizon is not built by one king's will alone. It is built by a machine of organization that can gather people, coordinate them, and keep them alive while they work. That machine is the Old Kingdom at its strongest. But machines can falter.

By the late Old Kingdom, multiple pressures appear to strain the system. Provincial elites gain power. The costs of maintaining monumental projects and centralized distribution rise. Climatic variability may have affected Nile floods in some periods, and a few bad years can shake confidence in a system built on predictable renewal. The political outcome is fragmentation in what later historians call the **First Intermediate Period** (roughly **c. 2181–2055 BCE**), when centralized authority weakens and regional powers contest control.

It would be easy to tell this as a moral tale: centralized order collapses, chaos follows, then stability returns. The reality is messier. Fragmentation can be violent and insecure, but it can also foster local resilience and new forms of power. Egypt does not stop being Egypt. It reorganizes.

The **Middle Kingdom** (commonly **c. 2055–1650 BCE**) emerges from reunification efforts centered in the south, often associated with rulers from Thebes who reassert control over the corridor. The Middle Kingdom is sometimes remembered as a period of administrative refinement and cultural confidence. The state strengthens its reach, stabilizes landholding, and invests in infrastructure. Literature flourishes in ways that later Egyptians admire as classic. But the Middle Kingdom is also a period when Egypt looks hard at its borders, especially in the south. Because Egypt's continuity is never only internal. It is shaped by Nubia.

To the south, along the Nile beyond the First Cataract, lie the worlds that Egyptians call **Nubia**, a region with its own cultures, polities, and traditions. Nubia is not a blank space on Egypt's map. It is a corridor of exchange, conflict, and deep interdependence. The south offers what Egypt values intensely: **gold**, along with cattle, ivory, ebony, and access to deeper African trade networks. Egyptians also fear the south at times, not as an abstract threat but as a real frontier where raiding, resistance, and rival authority are possible.

In the Middle Kingdom, Egypt builds a chain of fortresses in Lower Nubia, at places such as **Buhen** and **Semna**, designed to control movement along the river and project power. These are not only military posts. They are customs points. They are eyes and hands of the state, watching caravans, tracking goods, monitoring who crosses and when.

Imagine a border trade scene at the cataracts. Boats can't simply glide through the rapids. Cargo must be shifted, carried around obstacles, reloaded. Here, the state becomes physical: officials counting, scribes noting, guards watching. Nubian traders bring goods north, and Egyptians bring goods south, and both sides measure each other with the careful attention of people who know that exchange is never purely friendly. A bar of gold is wealth. It is also leverage. A shipment of grain can be generosity. It can also be dependence.

Egypt's northern and eastern connections matter too. By the late Middle Kingdom and into the **Second Intermediate Period (c. 1650–1550 BCE)**, Egypt faces new political realities in the delta, including the rise of rulers often called the **Hyksos**, who establish power in parts of northern Egypt. Egypt is not conquered into oblivion, but it is challenged, and that challenge reshapes military and political strategies. When Egypt reunifies again, it does so with sharper tools and a broader horizon.

That reunification opens the **New Kingdom** (commonly **c. 1550–1070 BCE**), Egypt's great age of empire and international diplomacy. This is the period when Egypt's monuments shift in emphasis from pyramids to vast temple complexes and rock-cut tombs, when armies march beyond the Nile valley into the Levant, and when the pharaoh is not only a divine ruler at home but a player in a multi-empire world.

You can hear the New Kingdom's tone in its temples. At **Karnak** and **Luxor**, at countless sanctuaries along the river, stone becomes a language of power and devotion. Reliefs show kings smiting enemies, offering to gods, receiving life and kingship symbols from divine hands. Temple building is piety, but it is also economics. Temples hold land, employ workers, store grain, and distribute rations. They become institutions with their own weight inside the state.

At the same time, Egypt's foreign policy becomes more complex than simple conquest. The

New Kingdom participates in a system of letters, gifts, marriages, and treaties that ties it to other major powers. The **Amarna Letters**, from the 14th century BCE, preserve a world where rulers address each other as "brother," exchange gold and luxury goods, and negotiate alliances and grievances through formal correspondence. Diplomacy is a kind of warfare conducted with words and prestige rather than arrows.

War still matters, and it matters at scale. Egypt's conflict with the Hittite empire culminates in famous events such as the **Battle of Kadesh** (often dated around **1274 BCE** under **Ramesses II**) and later a peace treaty, among the earliest surviving international treaties in recorded history. These moments are remembered partly because they were dramatic, and partly because they reveal a truth about the era: Egypt is now operating in a crowded geopolitical field, where power is balanced and contested rather than assumed.

Nubia remains central in the New Kingdom, but the relationship shifts. Egypt extends deeper control southward for long stretches, extracting gold and projecting authority, often through offices such as the "Viceroy of Kush." Yet control is never simply one-way. Nubians serve in Egyptian armies, participate in trade, and live within the imperial system, while Nubian identity and power persist and later rise spectacularly in periods after Egypt's New Kingdom zenith. The border is not a wall. It is a membrane.

Through all these phases, Egypt's continuity is real but not magical. The state endures because it is adapted to its corridor geography, because it can move resources along the river, because its ideology ties political authority to cosmic order, and because its institutions can regenerate after crisis. But the same features that enable continuity also create repeating tensions. Monumental projects demand surplus and labor. Surplus and labor demand administration and extraction. Extraction generates inequality and resentment. Border control creates wealth and conflict. Temples gain power that can rival kings. Periods of fragmentation return when the system's balance slips.

Return to the tomb inscription where we began. The words ask for bread and beer for the dead, as if the afterlife is sustained the way the worker village was sustained: through rations and order. That is not a coincidence. In Egypt, eternity is imagined through the logic of the state. The king is divine because order must be guaranteed. The temple is vast because the gods must be honored to keep the river's rhythm steady. The dead must be named because memory is a form of survival, and survival is the deepest promise a stable corridor can make.

Outside, the Nile continues its slow movement north. Boats move with it, carrying grain, stone, letters, soldiers, and rumors. At the southern border, traders watch the current and calculate the safest crossing points. In a worker village, someone rises before dawn, shoulders aching, and returns to the day's labor because the monument above them must keep growing. Egypt lasts because it turns rhythm into power.

13

The Indus Mystery

At dawn, before the heat takes hold, the well is already busy. A ring of baked brick rises from the street like a collar around dark water. A rope creaks. A jar bumps against the side and comes up dripping, cool enough to fog the air for a moment before it turns into plain liquid again. Feet shuffle on the hard-packed lane. Someone steps aside to let another pass. The movements are practiced, almost courteous, because this happens every day, and it has to keep working. Water is not a luxury in a city. It is the first condition of being one.

A few paces away, a narrow drain runs along the edge of a house wall, covered in fitted bricks or stone slabs. It carries away the used water with the calm efficiency of something designed, inspected, repaired. Not a ditch that happens to exist, but infrastructure that assumes the city will still be here tomorrow.

This is the Indus world at its most distinctive: urban life built not around a visible king's throne, but around systems that make millions of small actions possible.

By roughly **2600 BCE**, cities in the Indus region enter what scholars often call the **Mature Harappan** phase, lasting until around **1900 BCE**. The two most famous sites, **Harappa** (in modern Pakistan, near the Ravi River) and **Mohenjo-daro** (in Sindh, near the Indus), are not the only cities, but they are the clearest statements of a shared urban logic. Across a wide region, from inland cities to coastal ports, communities build with standardized bricks, lay out streets with purposeful regularity, and invest extraordinary effort in water management and sanitation.

If Mesopotamia's earliest cities announce themselves with temple complexes and expanding bureaucracies, and Egypt announces itself with divine kingship carved into stone, the

Indus cities offer a different kind of announcement: order without obvious royal display.

Walk through Mohenjo-daro in your mind and you feel it in the layout. Streets are often arranged in a grid-like pattern, with main avenues and smaller lanes branching off. Buildings are constructed of baked brick at a remarkable scale. Many houses include bathing areas and drains that connect to covered street sewers. Wells appear not only in monumental contexts but in neighborhoods, implying that access to water was a daily, distributed necessity rather than a privilege guarded behind palace walls. The famous "Great Bath" at Mohenjo-daro, a large lined basin with carefully managed water supply and drainage, suggests communal or ritual use, but the more telling detail is that it sits within a world where bathing and drainage are normal enough to be built into ordinary housing.

At Harappa, the story is similar: substantial architecture, standardized building materials, and evidence of planning that implies shared rules rather than ad hoc growth. Many Indus cities show a division between an elevated, more fortified or monumental area sometimes called a "citadel" and a larger "lower town." But what's striking is what we do *not* clearly see: huge royal tombs, giant statues of kings, palaces that dominate the skyline in the way Mesopotamian temples or Egyptian pyramids do. There are elite goods, and there were surely elites. No city without inequality has ever existed at this scale. But the Indus world does not broadcast monarchy in the same loud architectural voice. That raises a question historians still wrestle with: what kind of authority coordinated these cities?

The answer is cautious. We can infer organization because the evidence demands it. Standardized bricks, consistent weights, and urban infrastructure do not happen accidentally. They suggest shared norms enforced across generations. But whether those norms were imposed by kings, councils, merchant institutions, ritual authorities, or some combination remains uncertain. The Indus cities feel governed, but they do not reveal their governors in obvious portraits.

One of the clearest windows into their coordination is something small enough to fit in a palm: **standardized weights**. Across Indus sites, archaeologists have found sets of carefully shaped stone weights, often in chert, that conform to a shared system. In a marketplace, weights are more than tools. They are trust made physical. A standard weight allows a stranger to accept a measure without a fight. It allows contracts to be honored at a distance. It allows taxes, if taxes existed in a formal sense, to be assessed. It allows craft goods to be traded with consistency across a wide territory. The weights are a clue that the Indus world is not only urban, but commercial in a disciplined way.

That commerce is visible in craft production that reaches a level of refinement hard to imagine without specialized workshops and long training. Indus artisans produced fine beadwork, including carnelian beads often made through complex heating and drilling techniques. Shell working, ivory carving, metalworking, and pottery production appear across the civilization's footprint. Cotton textile production is widely associated with the Indus region as well, though textiles themselves rarely survive; the broader evidence suggests a sophisticated cloth economy. These crafts are not just local pride. They are exportable value, the kind of goods that can move along routes and return with materials a city cannot produce itself. And those routes did exist.

The Indus world is tied into wider networks that reach westward. Mesopotamian texts refer to **Meluhha**, a distant land many scholars associate with the Indus region, connected through maritime trade via the Persian Gulf. The material evidence includes Indus-style seals and goods found beyond the subcontinent and foreign materials found within Indus contexts. This does not mean a single "global economy" in the modern sense. But it does mean ships and caravans carried objects, and with them carried ideas about measurement, value, and reliability.

Here again a small object carries a large story: the **seal**. Indus seals are often carved from steatite and typically show an animal motif—sometimes the famous "unicorn"-like figure—alongside a short line of symbols. The seals likely functioned in identification and trade, marking goods or asserting authority over transactions. In other early civilizations, seals often accompany bureaucracy and property control. In the Indus, they suggest organized exchange and institution-backed trust, even if we cannot name the institution with certainty.

Then we meet the civilization's most stubborn silence: the script itself. Indus inscriptions are real, widespread, and consistent enough to be a writing system of some kind, but they are typically short, and no bilingual "Rosetta Stone" has yet been found to unlock them. Scholars disagree about what exactly the script encodes and even about how it functioned in daily life. Some argue it represents a full linguistic writing system; others propose it might be a more limited set of symbols tied to identity, commodities, or administrative categories. The cautious truth is this: we have signs, patterns, and repetition, but not enough context to translate confidently. The Indus cities speak to us through bricks, drains, and weights more clearly than through their symbols.

That silence matters because it forces discipline. It is tempting to fill a gap with a story. But the honest approach is to treat the Indus as a civilization we can describe in structure and practice without pretending we can hear its words. What we *can* hear, in a way, is the rhythm of daily life implied by the built environment.

A neighborhood well suggests routines of shared access. Covered drains suggest expectations of cleanliness and maintenance. Standardized bricks suggest regulated production, perhaps controlled kilns and supply chains. Streets laid with consistency suggest planning authorities that could impose and sustain layout decisions. None of this is casual. It implies people who understood that the city is not only houses. It is systems. And systems, as Mesopotamia already showed, can grow powerful and fragile at the same time.

By around **1900 BCE**, many Indus urban centers begin to change. This is often called the **Late Harappan** period, and it looks less like a sudden collapse and more like a long transition: cities decline in density, certain standardized practices weaken, and populations appear to shift toward smaller settlements and different regions, including movement eastward in some patterns. The old story of a single catastrophic invasion has largely fallen out of favor in serious scholarship. The evidence points instead toward multiple pressures: changing river courses, shifts in monsoon patterns and rainfall, ecological stress, and the reconfiguration of trade networks that linked Indus cities to distant partners.

When a city depends on coordinated water systems, stable supply, and predictable seasonal rhythms, climate and hydrology are not background. They are politics. If rivers shift or floods become less reliable, the cost of maintaining urban infrastructure rises. If long-distance trade falters, specialized production and elite exchange systems can be disrupted. If the balance between town and countryside changes, the city's ability to draw surplus and labor may weaken. None of these factors needs to be dramatic in a single year to be decisive over centuries.

So the Indus world does not simply vanish. It disperses, transforms, and leaves legacies that are harder to trace because they move into smaller-scale life, into regions where brick ruins do not pile as high.

Return to the well at dawn. The rope creaks again. Water rises again. In that moment, the Indus achievement feels less like a mystery and more like a choice repeated millions of times: to build systems that make dense life livable. To invest in infrastructure rather than spectacle. To standardize the invisible things—measures, bricks, drains—so that strangers can live close without constant breakdown. It is one answer to the problem of urban civilization, and it proves there was never only one path.

14

Bronze, Ancestors, Authority

The crack comes sharp, like a twig snapping in winter. A scapula, cleaned and dried, rests over coals until the bone tightens. The diviner lifts it with tongs, sets it on a flat surface, and presses a pointed tool into a prepared hollow. Heat meets pressure. The bone speaks in fractures.

In the lamplight, the lines look accidental at first. Then the trained eye finds the pattern. A question has already been carved nearby in neat, compact marks. Will the rain come on the next ten-day cycle? Will the king's toothache ease? Should the army march east? Will the ancestor accept the offering? The cracks are read, recorded, and sometimes later verified. The result is not only a prediction. It is a decision made legitimate.

In the world of early Chinese states, authority does not rest on force alone. It rests on a relationship with the dead, with the ancestors who are believed to lean close to the living world, and with a cosmic order that can be consulted, pleased, angered. War matters. Grain matters. Bronze matters. But what binds them into a state is a claim: that one lineage, one kingly house, has the right rituals and the right access to the unseen.

You can feel how different this is from the Indus cities you just left behind. The Indus world gives you planning without obvious royal display. Early China gives you the opposite: power announced through ritual, lineage, and controlled violence, made durable by bronze and made audible by writing. It begins before the famous names.

Long before the Shang kings cast their names into metal and scratched questions into bone, communities along the Yellow River and its tributaries were already building villages, storing grain, making pottery, raising pigs, and experimenting with social hierarchy. Over millennia, these communities grew more complex, their leaders finding new ways to gather surplus and organize labor. By the time you reach the late third and early second millennium BCE, the landscape is ready for a new kind of center.

That center is often associated with a site called **Erlitou**, in today's Henan province, dated broadly to around **c. 1900–1500 BCE**. Erlitou matters because it looks like a capital in the making: palatial foundations, workshops, elite goods, evidence of wide influence. It also matters because it sits at the heart of a long argument. Later Chinese historical tradition speaks of an early dynasty called the **Xia**, preceding the Shang. Some scholars have linked Erlitou to the Xia. Others urge caution, pointing out that written sources describing Xia were compiled much later and that archaeology cannot simply be forced to match later narrative. The careful truth is this: Erlitou represents early state-level complexity in the Yellow River region, whether or not we can confidently name it as "Xia."

What makes Erlitou and its contemporaries significant is not the label. It is the pattern. You see central buildings that suggest concentrated authority. You see craft specialization, including early bronze production. You see a society that can mobilize labor for large construction and control valuable materials. The ingredients of a state are already on the table.

Then the Shang arrive in the record with a different kind of clarity. By roughly **c. 1600 BCE**, the **Shang** period begins in the conventional chronology, lasting until around **1046 BCE**. Here, archaeology and writing begin to overlap in ways that allow a sharper picture, especially in the late Shang capital region near **Anyang** (also called **Yin**), associated with the last centuries of Shang rule, around **c. 1250–1046 BCE**.

Walk into a Shang city and you enter a world organized around a royal house that is both political command center and ritual engine. The king is not merely a war leader. He is the chief mediator with ancestors. The state is not merely a collection of taxes and soldiers. It is a lineage that claims cosmic backing, expressed through offerings, divination, and monumental craft.

Bronze is the material that makes this visible. A Shang bronze vessel is heavy in the hands, dense with metal and meaning. It is not made for everyday cooking. It is made for ritual: to hold wine, to present offerings, to mark a family's standing and the king's favor. The surfaces are covered in stylized masks and swirling designs that seem to move when firelight hits them. Casting such vessels requires technical skill and organized labor: mining and transporting copper and tin, controlling fuel supplies, managing foundry teams, maintaining molds. The Shang did not simply "have bronze." They built institutions that could command it. And because bronze is scarce and valuable, controlling it becomes controlling power.

Imagine a foundry yard near a palace precinct. The air smells of charcoal and hot clay. Molds are laid out like shells waiting to be filled. Workers move in disciplined sequences, because molten metal does not forgive confusion. A foreman checks a mold's fit. Someone stokes the furnace. When the pour begins, it is fast and irreversible. The vessel that emerges will become a sacred object, a political gift, a symbol of legitimate status. This is the state at work: taking raw material from the earth and turning it into authority that can be displayed and inherited.

War is the other engine, and the Shang are frank about it. Oracle bone inscriptions do not only ask about weather and harvest. They ask about raids, battles, enemies, captives. They record sacrifices and the outcomes of campaigns. The Shang king leads military expeditions against rival groups and polities, and victory feeds the ritual system: captives can become laborers, wealth can become offerings, and the king's success can be framed as ancestor-supported legitimacy. Violence is not separate from belief. It is braided into it.

The chariot arrives as part of this war system, likely influenced by wider Eurasian developments. By the late Shang, chariots and horses appear in elite contexts, tied to warfare and prestige. A chariot is not just a vehicle. It is an expensive military technology that requires trained horses, specialized craftsmen, and coordinated tactics. It concentrates power in the hands of those who can afford and manage it.

So the Shang state hardens into a pattern: a royal lineage at the center, commanding bronze, commanding war, commanding ritual, anchoring itself through an ancestor cult that is not merely family religion but state ideology.

And then comes writing in its most startling early form. The oracle bones. These are not literary texts. They are administrative and ritual records carved into bone and turtle shell, asking questions that matter to governance. They contain dates, names, offerings, outcomes. Over time, they build a picture of a court that runs on scheduled divination, on the management of uncertainty through controlled consultation with the unseen. The king's decisions are not presented as personal whims. They are framed as responses to ancestral guidance.

This matters because writing here is not merely record-keeping like the Mesopotamian ration tablet, though there is overlap in function. It is also a technology of legitimacy. The question and the crack together become a public proof that the decision was anchored in more than human desire.

You can see how this might stabilize rule. You can also see its vulnerability. If floods come despite divination, if harvests fail, if enemies win, the same system that legitimizes the king can begin to implicate him. If ancestors are displeased, perhaps the king is at fault. If the cosmic order is disturbed, perhaps the lineage has lost its right to rule. That is where the next transition becomes possible.

Around **1046 BCE** (traditional dating), the **Zhou** defeat the Shang and establish a new dynasty that will shape Chinese political thought for millennia. The Zhou do not only conquer. They explain conquest. They introduce a concept that will echo through later history: the **Mandate of Heaven**.

The Mandate of Heaven is a political theology with sharp edges. It says that Heaven (Tian), a moral-cosmic force, grants legitimacy to a ruler who governs properly. If a dynasty becomes corrupt, oppressive, or incompetent, Heaven can withdraw its mandate and grant it to another house. In practice, this doctrine provides a powerful justification for rebellion and replacement, but it also sets a standard that rulers must publicly honor. It turns history into a moral ledger.

The Zhou are careful in how they frame the Shang's fall. They do not deny the Shang's rituals and ancestors as meaningless. They argue that the Shang failed in virtue, that they lost alignment with Heaven's order, and that Zhou rule is therefore legitimate. It is a new kind of claim: legitimacy that can, in theory, be lost.

This is not modern democracy, and it does not prevent brutality. But it does establish a principle that later generations will return to whenever a dynasty weakens: famine, rebellion, invasion, corruption. Was the mandate withdrawn? The idea becomes a lens through which crisis is interpreted.

The Zhou also face a practical problem immediately after conquest: how do you control a large territory without a modern bureaucracy?

Their solution is an order often described, somewhat loosely, as feudal. The Zhou kings distribute lands and titles to relatives and allies, creating a network of regional lords bound by ritual obligations, tribute, and military support. In Chinese terms, later thinkers describe this as a

fengjian system: enfeoffment and hierarchical bonds. The effect is to extend Zhou influence outward through kinship and alliance, turning the royal house into the apex of a tiered political landscape.

You can see how this would look on the frontier. A garrison sits near a river crossing at the edge of cultivated land. The walls are not grand. They are practical: packed earth, timber, watch platforms. Soldiers rotate through duties that are mostly waiting, mostly watching. They repair palisade posts, drill with spears, patrol the nearby fields, and keep an eye on the movement of people beyond the zone of direct Zhou settlement. Some of those people trade. Some raid. Some negotiate. The frontier is not a line. It is a living space where authority is tested daily.

For a young officer, life is a mixture of boredom and sudden fear. Supplies arrive irregularly. The local lord's authority must be asserted without provoking constant revolt. Messages travel back toward the center with delays and distortions. In such conditions, ritual and hierarchy are not decorations. They are tools of cohesion. Oaths, ceremonies, and kin ties help hold a far-flung network together when physical force is stretched thin.

Bronze continues to matter in the Zhou world, but the emphasis shifts. Shang bronzes often dazzle as expressions of a powerful ritual court. Zhou bronzes increasingly become documents as well as objects. Inscriptions appear inside vessels, recording gifts, honors, and events. A bronze vessel becomes a permanent statement: the king recognized this lineage, granted this land, affirmed this bond. Metal holds memory the way clay tablets do in Mesopotamia and stone inscriptions do in Egypt. Different medium, similar function. Authority is made durable by being made legible.

This is an important continuity across early civilizations. As societies grow, they invent ways to store social facts outside the mind: who owes what, who belongs where, who holds rights, who has been honored, who has been cursed. The archive can be clay, bone, stone, or bronze. The goal is the same: to make power persist.

Yet the Zhou order is also unstable in its own way. A network of enfeoffed lords can expand quickly and hold large territories with limited central bureaucracy, but it creates semi-autonomous power centers. Over time, regional lords grow strong, local identities harden, and loyalty to the center becomes negotiable. The very system that spreads Zhou authority contains the seeds of later fragmentation and competition, which will become central to later Chinese history in the Eastern Zhou period and beyond.

Erlitou and its world show early state formation taking shape, even as we argue about names. The Shang show a mature Bronze Age state where ritual, war, bronze, and writing fuse into a powerful lineage-based order. The Zhou show conquest reframed as moral legitimacy through the Mandate of Heaven, and governance extended through a tiered political system grounded in kinship, oaths, and ritual hierarchy.

Across these centuries, early China demonstrates a distinctive route to state power. The state is not only an administrative machine. It is a ritual system. It organizes time through divination cycles and ceremonial calendars. It organizes society through lineage and rank. It organizes violence through campaigns sanctified by ancestral approval. It organizes memory through inscriptions that outlast the living.

Return to the oracle bone. The diviner's crack has been read. The answer has been recorded. The decision moves outward through the court, through messengers, through officers at distant posts, until it becomes action in fields and on roads. Somewhere a bronze vessel is being cast, its mold ready to receive molten metal. Somewhere a frontier garrison watches the horizon and tries to hold a fragile order in place.

15

Sea Worlds, Land Wars

The harbor smells like pitch, salt, and wet rope. A merchant ship sits low in the water, heavier than it looks from shore. Men on the dock strain as a sling tightens around a copper ingot shaped like an animal hide, its edges rounded from handling. Another comes up behind it. Then another. The metal flashes briefly in the sun before it disappears into shadowed storage.

Not far away, jars are rolled into place—oil, wine, resin. A bundle of raw glass the color of deep water is passed hand to hand as if it might break into riches. Someone checks the tally marks scratched on wood or pressed into soft clay.

Someone else watches the horizon, because in this world the sea is a road, and roads can be raided. The cargo is not just wealth. It is the bloodstream of an age.

In the Late Bronze Age, roughly **1600–1200 BCE**, the eastern Mediterranean becomes a connected zone held together by palace economies. The palaces are not only royal residences. They are warehouses, workshops, armories, and accounting offices. They take in grain, wool, oil, timber, and metal. They turn those inputs into soldiers, ships, luxury goods, and diplomatic gifts. They move materials across the sea and across mountain passes. They make war possible, and they make peace profitable. And because they are so efficient at connection, they create a new kind of fragility: when the network breaks, everything breaks quickly.

You can begin on **Crete**, where the sea seems less like a boundary than a home. By around **2000 BCE**, complex centers on Crete grow into what we call the **Minoan** world, named later from myth, not from a name the people wrote for themselves. Palatial sites like **Knossos, Phaistos, Malia**, and **Zakros** develop storage magazines packed with huge pithoi jars, workshops, and ceremonial spaces. The island's position makes it a natural hinge between the Aegean, Egypt, and the

Levant. Crete cannot produce everything it wants, especially metals. But it can produce what networks reward: finely made craft goods, oils, textiles, and ships that can carry them.

Minoan power is visible in architecture and art, not in massive fortification walls. Frescoes show leaping bulls and sea creatures, a world where movement and ritual feel bound together. The palaces look open in ways that later fortress-cities do not. That openness has inspired romantic stories of peaceful seafarers. The evidence is more cautious. Minoans certainly traded widely and built impressive maritime connections; whether they dominated the sea as a formal "thalassocracy" is harder to prove. But their economy clearly depended on sea lanes, and their palaces clearly organized production and storage at scale.

They also wrote. Yet their script—**Linear A**—remains undeciphered. We see signs, lists, repeated patterns. We can identify that they were keeping accounts. But the language stays behind a closed door. Like the Indus script, it demands humility. We can describe the machine without pretending to hear every word it spoke.

Crete's world is not isolated from disaster. Around **1600 BCE**, the volcanic eruption at **Thera (Santorini)** sends shockwaves—literal and cultural—through the Aegean. Exact dating is debated, and the eruption's impacts on Crete are still argued: tsunami, ash, disrupted trade, psychological shock. What is clear is that it lands in an already complex era, and complex systems do not absorb shocks easily.

In the centuries that follow, power in the Aegean shifts. By around **1450 BCE**, many Cretan palatial sites are destroyed or reorganized, and **Mycenaean Greeks** from the mainland appear to take over Knossos and incorporate parts of the island into their own administrative world. This is not a neat conquest story with one day of collapse and the next day of order. It is an era of transitions, regional variation, and power rebalancing. But the direction is unmistakable: the center of gravity moves toward the Greek mainland.

On the mainland, the Mycenaean world rises in a different mood. Where Crete's palaces often look outward and open, Mycenaean centers announce themselves with stone and height.

At sites like **Mycenae, Tiryns, Pylos, Thebes**, and later **Athens** in its own way, palatial complexes sit behind thick walls. The architecture is meant to impress and to endure. The kings' halls—the **megaron** rooms—center power in a single commanding space. Elite burials early in this era, like the shaft graves at Mycenae (from around **1600 BCE**), glitter with gold, weapons, imported goods. The mainland is plugged into the same international economy, and its elites make sure everyone can see it.

Here, writing becomes audible in a way it was not on Crete, because the Mycenaeans use **Linear B**, a script adapted from earlier Aegean writing that records an early form of Greek. We know this because Linear B was deciphered in the twentieth century, and what it reveals is telling: not heroic epics, but administration.

A Linear B tablet is small, almost rude in its plainness. It was never meant to last. It was meant to be used, checked, and discarded. The reason we have them is brutal and accidental: palace fires baked the clay hard, preserving the records at the moment the system failed.

Picture an inventory tablet from **Pylos**. It is not poetry. It is a list of goods and obligations: quantities of grain, allocations of wool, rations for workers, distributions of bronze to smiths. It shows a palace economy that does not merely collect tribute; it organizes production. It turns raw wool into cloth through controlled labor. It turns stored grain into fed crews. It turns bronze into weapons. It turns accounting into power.

This is where the palace economy's logic becomes clear. The palace sits at the top of a hierarchy, and it reaches into the countryside through officials, collectors, and workshops. It does not replace local life entirely; farmers still plant and harvest, herders still move animals. But the palace overlays that life with demands and channels. If you are a smith, the palace might supply your bronze and expect your output. If you are a weaver, the palace might supply wool and claim finished textiles. If you are a soldier, the palace might provide rations and equipment in return for service.

And always, the sea is present. Mycenaean ships move goods across the Aegean and beyond. Their pottery appears widely in eastern Mediterranean contexts, a sign of both trade and cultural reach. The sea carries olive oil, wine, perfumed resins, and crafted goods. It carries people too: envoys, brides, mercenaries, captives.

On land, chariots shape how elites fight and how they imagine themselves. The chariot is expensive. It demands trained horses, specialized craftsmen, and a supply chain of wood, leather, metal fittings, and skilled drivers. It is not simply a weapon. It is a system. In the Late Bronze Age, chariots become a marker of elite military identity across much of the Near East and parts of the

Aegean world. They allow rapid strikes on open ground and create a battlefield logic where mobility and prestige matter alongside brute infantry force.

But the Aegean is only half the story. Across the water and over the mountains, in **Anatolia**, a land empire is building its own version of palatial power with a sharper legal and diplomatic edge: the **Hittites**.

Centered at **Hattusa** in central Anatolia, the Hittite state grows from an Old Kingdom (often dated from around **1650 BCE**) into an imperial power in the Late Bronze Age, especially from the **14th–13th centuries BCE**. The Hittites sit astride crucial corridors connecting the Aegean world, the Levant, and Mesopotamia. They do not rely on sea lanes the way Crete does. They rely on roads, passes, vassal relationships, and archives.

Hittite statecraft is famous because of its paperwork and treaties. Where Mycenaean tablets tell you what the palace counted, Hittite documents tell you how the palace negotiated.

Treaties survive in Hittite archives that specify obligations between the Hittite king and subordinate rulers: loyalty, tribute, military support, and the penalties for betrayal. The language is formal, repetitive, and revealing. It shows a state that understands power not only as conquest but as managed hierarchy. And at the top sits a king who is not only a war leader but a diplomat in a world of "Great Kings."

By the Late Bronze Age, major powers treat each other as peers in a system that includes Egypt, the Hittites, Babylon, Assyria, and others. Diplomacy runs on gifts, marriages, letters, and carefully calibrated insult. A shipment of gold is not merely generosity. It is a statement about relative status. A princess sent in marriage is not romance. It is an alliance sealed in bloodlines. A delay in sending promised gifts can sour relations as much as a border raid. You can feel the texture of this international world in a treaty fragment.

After the battle at **Kadesh** around **1274 BCE** between **Ramesses II** of Egypt and the Hittite king (often associated with **Muwatalli II** at the time), the conflict does not end with a clean victory. Instead, it moves toward diplomacy. A peace treaty is concluded later, commonly dated to around **1259 BCE** under **Hattusili III** and Ramesses II. The treaty survives in versions from both sides, a reminder that even peace is a matter of narrative control. It includes promises of non-aggression and mutual support, framed in the language of gods and oath. It is an admission that the Late Bronze

Age is not only a world of raids and sieges, but a world where war has become too costly to be constant.

Meanwhile, goods keep moving. A ship's cargo can tell you what politics only implies. A famous example from this world is the **Uluburun shipwreck**, dated to the **14th century BCE**, found off the coast of modern Turkey. Its cargo reads like a catalog of the international Bronze Age: copper ingots, tin, glass, ivory, exotic woods, jewelry, and finished luxury items. You don't need to treat any single ship as "typical" to grasp the larger point. Networks had become dense enough that a single vessel could carry the materials of multiple regions in one floating archive.

All of this makes the Late Bronze Age look powerful, sophisticated, and stable. It is also exactly the kind of system that can fail in cascading ways. Because palace economies are strong, they centralize. Because they centralize, they depend on smooth flows: of grain into storerooms, of bronze into armories, of tin from far sources, of timber for ships and chariots, of skilled labor kept fed and loyal, of trade routes kept open. The stronger the network, the more catastrophic its disruption.

The precursors to collapse do not arrive with one trumpet blast. They show up as stress. A poor harvest year means a palace must distribute more from storage or risk unrest. A disrupted trade corridor means a foundry cannot get tin, and bronze production stutters. A rival power pressures a frontier, forcing the palace to mobilize chariot forces and garrisons, draining resources. Internal politics can fracture court cohesion. Earthquakes can damage walls and ports. Drought patterns, still debated in detail, may have strained multiple regions near the end of the Bronze Age. None of these on its own is destiny. Together, they can turn a highly interconnected world into a brittle one.

By around **1200 BCE**, many Late Bronze Age centers across the eastern Mediterranean experience upheaval: palaces burn, cities are abandoned or reduced, trade networks contract, and political orders reconfigure. The causes remain debated. Invasions and migrations by groups later labeled "Sea Peoples" appear in Egyptian sources, but even there they look less like a single invading nation and more like a symptom of wider instability: displaced groups, opportunistic raiders, collapsing allies, desperate movements. Scholars argue over how much weight to assign to warfare, drought, internal revolt, and system failure. What is hard to deny is the pattern: complex palace networks that took centuries to build can unravel quickly when their dependencies snap. And the evidence of that unravelling is often preserved in fire.

In Mycenaean Greece, the Linear B tablets survive because palace archives burned. The clay baked hard. The records freeze the system at the moment it fails: lists unfinished, allocations recorded, obligations pending. In Anatolia, Hattusa's archives preserve treaties and letters that show a state managing tensions right up to the edge of change.

The Aegean and Anatolia show how palaces can turn geography into power: Crete leveraging the sea, Mycenaean Greece fortifying and counting, the Hittites negotiating and commanding corridors. Chariots and bronze bind elites into a shared military culture. Diplomatic gift exchange turns luxury into politics. Treaties formalize relationships in a world that cannot afford constant war. But the very success of this system creates its vulnerability. When trade becomes lifeblood, disruption becomes trauma.

Return to the dock where the copper ingots were lifted from the ship. The men keep working. The tallies are checked. The goods disappear into storage. Somewhere inland, another palace is sending out wool and demanding cloth in return. Somewhere in Anatolia, a scribe copies a treaty clause carefully, because one wrong sign can turn an oath into an insult. Somewhere on a frontier, a garrison watches the road and waits for a caravan that is late.

Late is how collapse begins to feel. First as inconvenience. Then as shortage. Then as fear. And beyond the palaces, beyond the kings who exchanged gifts and threats, a larger question is waiting: what happens when the grand systems fall and ordinary people have to rebuild life from the fragments?

16

Civilization Off the Map

The mound rises out of flat land like a thought made physical. From a distance it looks natural, a gentle swell against the horizon. Up close you can see the truth in the layers: basket-load after basket-load of earth carried and poured, packed and shaped, season after season. The air is thick with insects and river damp. People climb the slope in a slow line, not because it is hard to walk but because the moment asks for a certain pace. At the top, the world opens—water channels, forest edges, distant smoke from camps—an entire landscape made legible from this one lifted place.

No king's name is carved here. No city wall encloses it. No palace archive counts rations in clay. Yet the mound is not an accident, and it is not small. It is coordination in a language older than writing: labor gathered, time organized, meaning agreed upon strongly enough that people spend their most precious resource—work—on something that does not feed them directly.

This is the warning against a lazy map of "civilization." If you only look at the classic river states—Mesopotamia, Egypt, the Indus, early China—you can start to believe that complex society has one birthplace and one shape: cities on big rivers, rulers in palaces, scribes in offices. But the ancient world was wider than those corridors, and complexity had more than one grammar.

Across deserts and savannas, across temperate forests and coastlines, across mountains and oceans, people built systems that were intricate, wealthy, and powerful—sometimes without cities, sometimes without writing, sometimes without obvious kingship. They did it by leaning into the advantages their environments offered: mobility rather than walls, ritual centers rather than palaces, trade routes rather than canals, textiles rather than stone, seafaring rather than fields. The result was not "primitive" life waiting to become a state. It was alternative sophistication.

Begin in the middle of a continent that textbooks too often treat as empty: the Sahara. Today the Sahara is a wall of heat and sand. In earlier millennia it was, at times, something else—greener, dotted with lakes and grasslands, traversed by people who herded cattle and left rock art and burial markers across places that now look uninhabitable. By the time we enter the later fourth and third millennia BCE, that greener world is shrinking. The long drying trend pushes people toward the Nile valley, toward the Mediterranean coast, and toward the Sahel—the belt south of the desert where savanna and seasonal rivers offer a different kind of stability.

This movement does not simply "remove" people from the Sahara. It reorganizes networks. In a corridor world, power often sits where water is. In a desert-edge world, power often sits where movement can be managed: at wells, passes, seasonal grazing routes, and chokepoints where salt, copper, and other scarce resources can be exchanged. Communities here become experts in logistics without bricks—knowing when to travel, where water will hold, how to move animals and goods across distances that punish mistakes. Mobility becomes infrastructure. Kinship becomes a road system. A caravan is not only commerce; it is survival strategy.

Along the Sahara–Sahel interface, this produces societies that can concentrate people and labor in bursts: seasonal gatherings, ritual centers, fortified settlements in some cases, and exchange hubs where goods and marriages move together. It is not always "urban" in the river-state sense, but it is organized and consequential. The desert does not erase complexity. It selects for a different kind.

Now shift to a different landscape that taught humans to think in routes: Bronze Age Europe. BEurope in the third and second millennia BCE is not a blank prelude to Greece and Rome. It is a continent of metal, forests, rivers, and coastlines threaded by exchange. Copper, tin, gold, and amber pull people into networks that are as strategic as any canal system. Bronze requires a relationship between distant places because copper and tin are rarely found together in convenient abundance. If you can't control both, you must control routes—or at least maintain alliances with those who do.

Imagine a packet of metal on the move: a bar of copper from the Alps or the Balkans, a bundle of tin moving from far sources, a piece of amber glowing like trapped sunlight from the Baltic. These materials travel along river corridors like the Danube, along coastal routes, and through mountain passes. They pass through hands that specialize: miners, smelters, smiths, traders, guards. Along the way, metal becomes not only tools and weapons but social hierarchy. A bronze sword is a fighting instrument. It is also a badge. A gold ornament is not edible. It is a claim.

This is how European complexity often looks: not early empires with archives, but warrior elites, fortified hilltops, long-distance alliances, and ritual deposits in bogs and rivers—offerings that suggest wealth being converted into sacred legitimacy. Where Mesopotamia shows you a city-state balancing storerooms and debt, Bronze Age Europe shows you networks balancing prestige, violence, and exchange. Different machinery, same human pressures: who controls the scarce, who organizes the many, who convinces others to follow.

Now cross to the Andes, where complexity learns to speak in fiber and altitude. Along Peru's arid coast, the ocean is a reliable engine. Cold currents feed rich fisheries, and those fisheries can support dense populations even where rainfall is scarce. Inland, rivers cut green valleys through desert. Up in the highlands, different ecologies stack like layers of a cake—each with its own crops, animals, and risks. In this world, connection is vertical as much as horizontal: coast to valley to plateau.

Here, one of the earliest striking patterns is the rise of monumental architecture in coastal and valley regions by the late fourth and third millennia BCE—large communal buildings and planned centers built without the familiar markers of "civilization" like pottery in some early contexts. The details vary by site and scholars debate how centralized these societies were, but the broader message is hard to miss: you can build monuments and coordinate labor on a grand scale without copying Mesopotamia's script or Egypt's divine kingship.

And the Andes offer a different primary medium of wealth and meaning: textiles. An Andean textile is not decoration on the margins of life. It is technology, identity, and power woven together. Cotton from coastal zones and fibers from highland animals can be turned into cloth that stores labor the way grain stores calories. Cloth can be traded, gifted, displayed, inherited. Patterns can mark affiliation and rank. A finely made textile is portable prestige, light enough to carry across mountains, valuable enough to bind alliances.

Picture a piece of cloth unfolding in sunlight at a meeting place between ecological zones. The weave is tight and even. The design is deliberate, repeating. The cloth's value is not only in its beauty but in the time it represents—hours, days, weeks of skilled work—compressed into something that can be carried and exchanged. In such a world, a caravan of llamas (in later phases where camelid herding and transport become central) is not merely transport. It is the stitching of a vertical economy, linking coast and highland, fish and tubers, cotton and wool, salt and stone.

The Andes show another path to complexity: not one great river corridor, but a ladder of environments connected by movement and reciprocity, with textiles as one of the primary currencies of status and obligation.

Now move to North America, where earth becomes ceremony. Long before cities like Cahokia, mound-building traditions appear in different regions and periods, sometimes as clusters of earthworks that gather people for ritual, exchange, and seasonal organization. A site like **Poverty Point** in the lower Mississippi Valley (flourishing roughly in the second millennium BCE) is often discussed as a major center: vast earthworks, ridges and mounds laid out with purpose, evidence of long-distance exchange in materials that traveled remarkable distances for the time.

Stand at such a place during a gathering and you can imagine the social physics without inventing a king. People arrive with stone from far sources, shells from coasts, pigments, crafted goods, and food prepared for a communal event. They trade. They feast. They arrange marriages. They settle disputes. They perform ceremonies that reaffirm belonging. The mound, again, is the anchor—a place that holds a community together even when the community is otherwise spread across forests, wetlands, and river channels.

This is complexity expressed as congregation rather than permanent urban density. The center is not necessarily a city where everyone lives year-round. It can be a ceremonial and exchange hub that becomes powerful precisely because it draws dispersed people into periodic unity. It creates a social map larger than any village's daily life.

Finally, follow the ocean routes that turn islands into stepping stones. In the western Pacific, beginning around the second millennium BCE, seafaring communities expand into new island worlds in a movement often associated with what archaeologists call the **Lapita** horizon. The signature is often found in pottery: carefully made vessels decorated with dentate-stamped patterns—tiny repeated impressions that create geometric designs. These pots appear across a wide arc of islands, tracking movement and connection across distances that would be impossible without sophisticated navigation, boatbuilding, and planning.

A Lapita pot shard on a beach tells a story as clearly as an obsidian blade far from a volcano. It says people crossed open water and brought traditions with them. It says they carried domesticated plants and animals into new ecologies, adapted gardens to island soils, and built networks across sea lanes. It says identity traveled with technique: the same stamping patterns repeating in places separated by hundreds or thousands of kilometers of water.

Seafaring societies face a different set of constraints than river states. Islands are small; resources can be limited; ecological mistakes can be fatal. This selects for careful management, social rules around land and reef use, and strong knowledge transmission. Navigation itself becomes a cultural treasure: star paths, wave patterns, bird movements, cloud shapes over distant land. Expansion is not just daring. It is disciplined expertise.

Look across all these worlds—Sahara corridors, European metal routes, Andean vertical systems, North American mound centers, Pacific seafaring—and the common thread is not a single "civilizational package." It is the ability to coordinate labor, manage scarcity, and create legitimacy.

Some societies did it through kingship and writing. Others did it through ritual gatherings and earthworks. Others through trade control and prestige goods. Others through boat technology and ecological rule-making. In every case, complexity is real, and it is locally engineered. And the consequences matter.

These "beyond the cradles" worlds fed larger systems too. African corridors and Sahelian edges would later become crucial to trans-desert exchange. European metals and maritime routes shaped Mediterranean dynamics. Andean networks laid the foundations for later highland and coastal states. North American mound traditions created long-distance exchange patterns and political imaginations that later societies would intensify. Pacific expansions transformed human geography, settling vast ocean spaces and building cultural worlds that could endure in relative isolation.

Return to the mound where we began. People descend as the ceremony ends, footsteps softening the slope. The mound remains, not as a palace but as proof: strangers can become a community long enough to build something that outlasts them. Somewhere else, a bronze ingot changes hands along a river. Somewhere in the Andes, a textile is folded and tied for travel. Somewhere on a Pacific shore, a pot breaks and a shard sinks into sand, waiting for a future that will call it evidence.

17

Forging the State

The clay tablet is small enough to be lost in a palm, yet it carries the weight of a harvest. In a storeroom that smells of dust and sour grain, someone has pressed signs into wet clay: measures, names, places, obligations. The list is practical, almost dull at first glance. So many baskets of barley from this village. So many jars of oil from that orchard. So many days of labor owed when the canal is dredged, when the wall is repaired, when the temple roof needs beams hauled up by rope.

It is not poetry. It is not a legend. It is a claim that reaches beyond one face-to-face conversation. It says the countryside will feed the center. It says the center has the right to ask. And it says there is a system that will remember if you don't pay.

That is where a state begins to come into focus, not as a flag or a palace, but as a set of capabilities that turn human life into an organized flow: resources, labor, obedience, and meaning moving through predictable channels.

The mistake people make, again and again, is to define "state" by stereotypes. A state is not automatically a city, though cities often help. A state is not automatically a king, though rulers often stand at the top. A state is not automatically writing, though writing makes the machine stronger. And a state is not automatically "civilization," as if everything outside its borders is only waiting to become one. A state is, at its core, a way of making power durable.

You can see it most clearly when you compare it to the worlds just behind us. In earlier chapters we've seen megasites without obvious monarchs, ceremonial centers without palaces, long-distance exchange without tariffs. Those worlds could be complex, wealthy, and coordinated. But they often relied on persuasion, kinship, ritual gatherings, and reputation systems that worked best when people could still leave, still vote with their feet, still dissolve a dispute by distance.

A state is what happens when leaving stops being the easy answer, and when someone builds tools to make staying, paying, and obeying routine. Start with the most basic capability: extraction and redistribution.

A state does not just receive gifts. It compels resources on a schedule. It can call it tax, tribute, corvée labor, offerings, dues. The word changes. The mechanism is the same. The state identifies households, fields, herds, or villages as sources of surplus and then insists that a portion be transferred to an institutional center.

That transfer can take many forms. In Mesopotamia, it often looks like grain and labor recorded on tablets, stored in temple and palace complexes, redistributed as rations to workers and soldiers. In Egypt, it looks like a corridor-state moving surplus along the Nile, feeding crews, temple staffs, and administrators while also financing stone-moving projects that dwarf ordinary village capacity. In Shang China, it looks like a royal lineage drawing goods and labor into a central ritual and military system, then returning prestige and protection to allied lineages, and punishment to enemies.

Redistribution is the part people remember fondly: the granary that opens in a bad year, the temple feast, the ration that arrives when your household is struggling. Extraction is the part people resent: the collector, the demand, the measurement that always feels a little unfair. A state is built on both. If it only extracts, it becomes a predator and invites revolt. If it only redistributes, it cannot sustain itself. The real art is managing the balance so that most people, most of the time, accept the bargain.

But even extraction and redistribution are not enough without the next capability: coercion.

Coercion does not always mean constant violence. Most successful states cannot afford constant violence; it is expensive and destabilizing. Coercion means the state holds a credible threat, and it can deploy it selectively enough that most compliance becomes routine.

That threat can be an army, a police force, a garrison, a fortified palace guard, or a network of allied elites obliged to bring fighters when summoned. In early states, armies often begin as organized extensions of existing war practices, then harden into standing institutions.

The details vary, but the principle is consistent: the state can compel bodies, not only goods.

You can feel that capability on a frontier where a watchtower stands over a road, or in the quiet authority of a soldier at a granary door. The countryside sees the same message everywhere: the center can reach you.

Coercion also includes the state's ability to punish. Punishment is not only a beating or an execution. It can be forced labor, seizure of land, loss of status, confiscation of goods, enslavement, exile. The exact forms differ, but punishment is the key that makes taxes collectable and debts enforceable. Without enforcement, a "tax list" is a wish. With enforcement, it becomes governance.

Then comes a capability that seems softer but is just as decisive: law and adjudication.

A society can have norms without a state. It can have elders, councils, mediation, feud systems. A state formalizes dispute resolution and claims a monopoly over legitimate judgment. It sets up courts, judges, officials, procedures, and penalties that can override private retaliation.

Now we are in a court room, not a modern one with polished wood, but an older space where judgment still feels intimate and dangerous. A farmer accuses a neighbor of moving a boundary marker after a flood shifted the channel. Another claims a loan was repaid, but the creditor presents a record. A widow petitions for a share of property that her husband's kin want to deny her. A merchant claims fraud in a weight measure at the market. The dispute is small enough to be personal, but large enough to matter. If the court rules one way, one household keeps land. If it rules another, that household loses a future.

Here is what makes it a state moment: the judgment is not simply negotiated between families. It is issued as an institutional decision, backed by enforcement. Even when courts are biased, even when elites manipulate them, the existence of a court shifts the political landscape. It turns conflict from a purely private struggle into something the center can regulate.

And it does something else, something subtle and enduring. It makes people think in categories the state can manage: legal person, property, debt, obligation, crime, punishment. Once you learn to see your life through those categories, the state has already sunk roots into your imagination. Which leads to the next capability: bureaucracy.

Bureaucracy is the state's nervous system. It is the network of offices, scribes, clerks, accountants, inspectors, messengers, warehouse managers, and record keepers who make the system run when the ruler is not present. A king can shout a command once. A bureaucracy can repeat it for decades.

This is why writing so often travels with states, even though states can exist without it. Writing allows storage of information beyond memory, standardization of orders, auditing of goods, and the creation of archives that outlast individual officials. But even where writing is limited or absent, bureaucracy can still exist as procedures, lists remembered by specialists, tokens, seals, and standardized measures. The Indus seals and weights hint at this: a world organized enough to require standards, even if we cannot read its symbols. Bureaucracy is also what makes the state scalable. A village chief can manage a few hundred people through personal authority. A state that spans valleys and coasts needs intermediaries and paperwork, or its orders dissolve as they travel.

Now add the final capability without which states rarely endure: ideology and legitimacy.

States cannot rule by force alone, not for long. The cheapest form of rule is the kind people consent to, or at least accept as normal. Legitimacy is the story a state tells about why its demands are justified.

Egypt tells it in the language of divine kingship and cosmic order: the pharaoh maintains balance and the Nile's rhythm is part of that sacred alignment. Shang China tells it through ancestors and divination: the king mediates between worlds, and decisions are authorized by the dead and the cosmos. The Zhou tell it through the Mandate of Heaven: rule is moral, and failure is proof of losing legitimacy. Mesopotamian kings tell it through temples, victory, and law codes that portray the ruler as the guarantor of justice.

A coronation ritual is where legitimacy becomes a public event rather than a private claim. Picture the moment: the ruler is presented before gods or their representatives, crowned or anointed, seated on a throne, given regalia that symbolizes more than personal power. Priests speak formulas. Officials bow. Gifts are exchanged. A crowd witnesses. The ritual does not merely celebrate authority. It manufactures it. It turns "this person is strongest" into "this person is rightful."

Even if the ruler took power through violence, coronation wraps that violence in meaning. It tells the population: order has returned. The future can be planned again. The taxes and labor demands now have a sacred or legal frame, which makes compliance more likely and revolt easier to label as sacrilege or treason.

Now step back and you can see why defining "a state" by stereotypes fails. A state does not have to look like Egypt's stone permanence or Mesopotamia's temple archives. It can be smaller, more mobile, less monumental. What matters is capability: can it extract resources reliably, enforce claims, adjudicate disputes, coordinate labor, maintain order through institutions, and justify itself through a legitimacy story strong enough to keep the machine from constantly tearing itself apart?

One more piece completes the picture: the city–countryside relationship. States feed on the countryside, but they also transform it. Cities and palace centers become magnets for surplus, labor, and specialized production. They also become markets, ritual hubs, and political theaters. The countryside is where most people live and where most food is produced. The state's central problem is to pull enough out of rural life to sustain the center without pushing rural communities into collapse or rebellion.

That balance shapes everything. Irrigation demands organized labor and maintenance. Roads and canals demand repair. Armies demand provisioning. Temples demand offerings. Courts demand fines. If extraction grows too heavy, people flee, resist, hide grain, sabotage records, or rally behind local leaders who promise relief. If extraction is too light, the center cannot fund protection or projects, and its prestige weakens.

This is why states are never only about rulers. They are about logistics and the countryside's willingness, grudging or sincere, to keep participating.

So what is a state *not*?

It is not simply "a big society." Many large societies organized themselves without a state monopoly over force. It is not simply "writing." Writing can exist in limited forms without clear state structures, and states can exist with minimal writing. It is not simply "monuments." Monuments can be built by complex foragers and ritual coalitions, as we saw. It is not even "a king." A powerful ruler without bureaucracy and extraction mechanisms may be a warlord, a chief, a charismatic leader, but not necessarily a stable state.

A state is the moment power becomes systemic. That system is never purely rational. It always contains contradictions. The same bureaucracy that prevents famine can deepen inequality. The same courts that reduce feuds can entrench elites. The same ideology that unifies can justify conquest. The same army that protects can become a threat. The same taxes that build roads can crush households in bad years.

And that leads to the next truth, the one states themselves often try to deny: states can fail. Because the more capabilities a state develops, the more dependencies it creates. It depends on predictable harvests, compliant collectors, loyal soldiers, functioning routes, stable legitimacy narratives. Disrupt one thread and the strain spreads. Disrupt several and the system begins to shed parts of itself: provinces break away, archives burn, garrisons mutiny, trade collapses, borders shift.

Return to the tax list tablet in the storeroom. The clay dries. The marks harden. For a moment, it looks like permanence. But it is only as permanent as the system behind it. If the collectors stop coming, the list becomes meaningless. If the granary empties, the rations stop. If the court is ignored, judgments are only words. If the king loses legitimacy, the coronation becomes a memory people mock. Collapse, in world history, is not the end of a story. It is the beginning of another kind of one.

18

When Systems Break

The storerooms are silent now. A row of giant jars lies on its side, cracked open, their mouths choked with ash. Grain has spilled and turned to a dark crust on the floor. The air smells of burned wood and something sour that was once oil. In the corner, where a clerk used to sit and count deliveries, clay tablets are scattered like dropped teeth. They were meant to be temporary. They survived only because the roof caught fire, the heat baked the clay, and the palace died fast enough to preserve its paperwork.

Outside, weeds are already pushing through the courtyard dust. A doorway stands open, its hinge twisted by heat. Beyond the wall the fields still exist, and the sea still glitters, and the seasons still turn. But the system that made this place matter is gone.

For centuries across the eastern Mediterranean, palace economies had turned the region into a connected machine. Ships moved copper and tin, oil and wine, luxury goods and letters. Fortresses guarded roads. Scribes kept lists. Kings exchanged gifts and threats. Chariots thundered across plains. It looked strong because it was organized. It looked stable because it was familiar.

Then, around **1200 BCE**—not in a single day, not for a single reason, not everywhere in the same way—the machine began to fail.

"Collapse" is a blunt word for what was, in reality, a chain reaction. In some places, cities burned and were abandoned. In others, palaces fell but villages persisted. Some regions saw sharp population drops; others saw shifts in settlement patterns rather than emptying. What ties these experiences together is not a universal apocalypse. It is a shared kind of disruption: the networks that had made palatial power possible became unreliable, and when they did, the institutions that depended on them lost their grip.

A palace is not just a building. It is an agreement enforced by logistics. It depends on harvests arriving as tax or tribute, on labor crews being fed, on trade routes delivering materials, on allies honoring treaties, on scribes keeping records that people accept as binding. When enough of those threads fray at once, the palace can burn even if no enemy breaks the gate. Sometimes it burns because its own people turn on it. Sometimes it burns because its soldiers are unpaid. Sometimes it burns because it is struck by outsiders drawn by the scent of stored wealth.

The late Bronze Age was especially vulnerable because it was deeply connected. Bronze itself is a clue. Copper and tin rarely sit conveniently together, so the metal economy depended on long-distance supply. Disrupt the flow of tin and the foundries stall. Disrupt the flow of grain and the workforce turns hungry. Disrupt the sea lanes and coastal cities lose their reason for being. A connected system can enrich everyone it touches. It can also fail like a row of dominos.

In the eastern Mediterranean, the list of places affected is long: Mycenaean palaces on the Greek mainland, many cities in the Levant, the Hittite capital region in Anatolia, and others. Some centers were destroyed; others contracted; others reorganized. Egypt, with its Nile backbone, did not vanish, but it faced pressure and a shrinking reach. The political map did not simply "go dark." It changed shape.

This is where the phrase "Sea Peoples" enters, and it needs careful handling. Egyptian inscriptions from the late New Kingdom describe groups arriving by sea and land, fighting battles, and threatening the delta. Later historians bundled these groups into a single label: Sea Peoples. It is tempting to imagine them as a unified invading nation that toppled civilizations like dominoes. The evidence suggests something more complex and more human: multiple groups on the move, some raiders, some displaced communities, some mercenaries, some opportunists, some refugees. In other words, not a single cause of collapse, but a symptom of a world already destabilizing.

When systems weaken, movement accelerates. People move because drought tightens pasture and harvest. People move because war destroys fields. People move because palaces that once paid soldiers and craftsmen cannot do so anymore. People move because a nearby region has fallen and violence spills across borders. Some movements are planned. Others are desperate. In the end, migration is rarely a simple story of one people replacing another. It is a mixing, a reshuffling, a series of bargains made under pressure.

Trade disruption sits at the center of this reshuffling. In the earlier age, a merchant could reasonably expect the next port to be open, the next treaty to hold, the next shipment of metal to arrive. When that confidence dies, long-distance exchange becomes riskier and more expensive. A ship's cargo becomes a target. A caravan needs guards it cannot afford. A coastal city that once thrived as a hub becomes exposed, and exposure invites predation. Even if the sea itself remains navigable, trust becomes scarce. And trust is what keeps markets alive.

You can see the human scale of this in the second scene, far from palace storerooms and royal inscriptions. A line of people moves along a road that is barely a road, more a worn strip through fields. They carry bundles wrapped in cloth, a few pots, a child's blanket, a tool that belonged to a father or a grandmother. Some walk barefoot because shoes were left behind in the rush. A cart creaks under what little can be saved. Ahead, smoke stains the horizon where their last home used to stand.

They are not "barbarians." They are families. They are refugees from a broken order.

They might be farmers whose local lord can no longer protect them. They might be craftsmen once attached to a palace workshop, now unanchored. They might be people pushed out by drought or pulled by rumors that a safer valley exists beyond the next ridge. They might be a mixed group, strangers forced into cooperation by necessity.

In a world like this, identity hardens and blurs at the same time. Hardens because people cling to what they know when everything else is uncertain. Blurs because displacement forces mixing: intermarriage, adoption, new alliances, new languages learned quickly for survival. The old labels on a diplomat's letter matter less than the reality of who can feed you and who will kill you.

This is the real landscape behind the "Sea Peoples" stories: a Mediterranean in motion. What emerges from the motion is not simply decline. It is reconfiguration.

In the Greek world, the fall of Mycenaean palaces means the disappearance of the palace's administrative writing, like Linear B, and a contraction of long-distance exchange. Settlements shift; some sites are abandoned; others persist at smaller scale. Later Greeks remembered a heroic age of kings and war, and they placed stories like the Trojan War on this horizon of disruption, mixing memory and myth. The archaeology suggests an era of fragmentation and local reorganization. It was harder to be a king when the palace economy that fed chariots and scribes had burned.

In Anatolia, the Hittite imperial structure breaks apart, and the political landscape becomes a patchwork of successor states and local powers. The old center loses its ability to command distant regions. New polities form, some building on older traditions, others mixing influences in ways that later historians struggle to neatly classify. The corridors remain. The orders change.

In the Levant, coastal and inland regions reconfigure as well. Trade does not die; it changes hands and routes. New city networks rise. Over time, groups and kingdoms that will matter in later centuries take clearer shape. This is not a single "people" stepping into an empty stage. It is a crowded, contested landscape where new institutions form because the old ones cannot be rebuilt in the same way.

Egypt, too, adapts. It fights off some threats, loses influence in others, and turns inward at times, focusing on the Nile core rather than imperial reach. The monuments remain, but imperial confidence does not.

And throughout this era, a new material begins to move from novelty to everyday usefulness: **iron**.

Iron was known earlier in small quantities in some contexts, but the broad spread of iron tools and weapons accelerates in the centuries after the Bronze Age disruptions, especially through the early first millennium BCE. The reasons are practical. Bronze depends on tin, and tin supply is vulnerable to trade disruption. Iron ore is more widely available in many regions, even if working iron well requires high heat and skilled technique. When long-distance networks wobble, a material you can source closer to home becomes attractive. Iron does not "replace" bronze overnight. Both coexist for a long time. But iron changes the economic geography of power. It reduces dependence on a few distant sources and makes tool production more locally achievable.

This is where the third scene matters: the village with new iron tools. A smith works under an awning, the ground dark with charcoal. The metal he holds looks ordinary, dull, nothing like the gleam of a bronze sword meant for a palace hall. But when he heats it and hammers it, you can see how it will change life. A plow point that holds its edge longer. A sickle that bites more cleanly. A knife that does not depend on imported tin. These are not royal treasures. They are household revolutions.

When iron tools spread, they don't just change warfare. They change farming. More durable tools can increase productivity. More accessible metal can expand who has access to weapons, which can make violence more widespread or more evenly distributed depending on the context. In some regions, this shift helps new kinds of armies form. In others, it empowers local elites who can arm followers. The technology does not dictate a single outcome. It opens possibilities.

And this is the deeper point. Collapse is not simply destruction. It is a filter. When large, centralized systems fail, what survives tends to be what can operate at smaller scales: village life, flexible networks, local leaders, portable skills. What returns tends to be what can be rebuilt under new constraints: new trade routes, new political bargains, new forms of legitimacy. Sometimes the result is less wealth at the top and more autonomy in the countryside. Sometimes it is more insecurity and more raiding. Often it is both, depending on where you stand.

People adapt because they must. They reuse stones from ruined palaces to build smaller walls. They turn abandoned storerooms into shelters. They relocate to defensible hills. They shift crops. They change the way they trade. They tell new stories that explain why the old order fell and why the new one deserves loyalty.

In the palace storeroom, the ration tablets remain as baked relics. They are evidence of a world that trusted lists and managed strangers through records. That world did not end because humans forgot how to count. It ended because the institutions that made counting meaningful could not survive simultaneous shocks: conflict, movement, disrupted trade, and possibly environmental stress layered over already tense politics.

Outside, on the road, the refugee line keeps moving. Those people carry fragments of the old world with them: skills, songs, grudges, techniques, seeds, gods. They seed the new world whether they intend to or not. And in the village, the iron tool bites into soil. It makes a clean sound, different from stone, different from bronze. It is not a promise of peace or progress. It is simply a new way to get through the year.

The Late Bronze Age does not "fall" into nothingness. It breaks, and from the pieces come new patterns: smaller kingdoms, new trade networks, fresh forms of warfare, new languages and identities taking shape, a Mediterranean that will eventually reconnect in different ways. Out of palaces come city-states and kingdoms of another kind. Out of broken treaties come new alliances. Out of bronze dependency comes iron opportunity. The storeroom stays abandoned, but the world does not stop.

Part IV

Axial Age & Classical Empires (c. 1200 BCE–200 CE)

19

Age of Iron

The dust hangs in the air like a second sky. Below a battered ramp of packed earth and timber, men lean into a wheeled frame sheathed in wet hides. Arrows thud into it and stick. Others bounce off and rattle away. The machine keeps creeping forward anyway, its weight shifting with every shove. From the wall above, defenders throw stones and firepots; the flames lick, then die against damp coverings. Somewhere behind the moving shield, iron-headed picks bite at masonry. Somewhere to the side, archers lay down a steady storm to keep heads down on the parapet. This is siege warfare as an industry. Not a heroic clash of champions, but a method—engineers, sappers, logistics, intimidation—applied until stone gives up.

By the early first millennium BCE, after the Late Bronze Age systems splintered, the eastern Mediterranean and Near East did not stay fragmented for long. The pieces reassembled into something harsher and more expansive, driven by a set of technologies and practices that traveled together: **iron tools and weapons, horses used at scale**, and **new ways of moving armies and supplies** over long distances. Iron did not magically create empires, and horses did not automatically win wars. But combined with disciplined organization, they widened the ceiling of what conquest could do.

The first great beneficiary was **Neo-Assyria**.

From the **ninth to the seventh centuries BCE**, Assyrian kings based at cities like **Kalhu (Nimrud)** and later **Nineveh** built a war machine that turned seasonal raiding into sustained imperial rule. Their armies did not rely solely on chariots, the old prestige weapon of Bronze Age elites. Chariots still existed, but cavalry and massed infantry mattered more and more. Horses became an engine of speed and shock. Mounted scouts could see farther and respond faster. Cavalry could pursue fleeing enemies and strike where chariots struggled, especially in uneven terrain. The empire could press outward not only because it fought well, but because it learned to **move**—to carry supplies, to keep roads open, to maintain garrisons, to return year after year until resistance collapsed.

Assyrian reliefs carved in palace halls show the method with brutal clarity: ladders against walls, battering rams, archers, prisoners marched away in lines. One famous moment comes in **701 BCE**, when **Sennacherib** besieged **Lachish** in the kingdom of Judah. The reliefs that celebrate the victory are propaganda, but they also record a reality: siegecraft had become systematic, and the psychological effect was part of the weapon. A city that watched a neighbor's walls fall understood what was coming.

Yet the most empire-changing Assyrian tool was not iron or a horse. It was administration fused to terror and logistics. Neo-Assyria refined the practice of turning conquered lands into provinces with officials who answered to the center. It demanded tribute and labor. It built and maintained roads and waystations. It made an example of resistance—and it moved people. **Deportations** were not an incidental cruelty; they were a strategy. Uprooting populations could break local power networks, repopulate strategic zones, and provide labor where the empire needed it. The human cost was immense, but the political logic was coldly effective: if identity and resistance are tied to place, then control the people by moving them.

Now step away from the siege ramp and walk into the countryside the empire depended on. A farmer in a frontier district does not experience "Neo-Assyria" as a map. He experiences it as schedules and demands. The harvest is weighed. The portion owed is non-negotiable. A son might be taken for labor on a road crew or service in a garrison. In good years, the empire's order can feel like protection: bandits suppressed, markets reachable, irrigation repaired. In bad years, it feels like a vise: the tax still comes when the granary is thin, and refusal is not a private choice. Empire is lived in the grain bin before it is seen in the palace relief.

Assyria's expansion also reshaped the sea. Along the eastern Mediterranean coast, **Phoenician** city-states—**Tyre, Sidon, Byblos**—thrived as maritime specialists. They did not build vast land empires like Assyria, but they built something that could outlast battlefield victories: networks. Their ships carried timber, textiles dyed with expensive purple, metal goods, glass, and crafted luxuries across the Mediterranean. They founded and supported colonies and trading outposts, the most famous being **Carthage**, traditionally dated to the late ninth century BCE. Wherever Phoenician trade went, it carried practical knowledge: shipbuilding, navigation, commercial methods—and writing systems that were easier to spread than complex scribal scripts. Empires could conquer coasts, but the sea still rewarded those who knew how to move quietly, quickly, and profitably between ports.

This mattered because empires are hungry for what they cannot make locally—especially metals, timber, and prestige goods that keep elites loyal. Phoenician networks fed that hunger. They also created alternatives. A coastal city tied into maritime trade can sometimes bargain with a land empire from a stronger position than its walls alone would suggest. Networks can be a form of leverage.

Assyrian power did not last forever. No power does. By the late seventh century BCE, Assyria faced mounting pressure: overstretch, internal succession strains, and powerful enemies. In **612 BCE**, a coalition including **Babylonians** and **Medes** took **Nineveh**. The great imperial center fell, and the region's political gravity shifted again—rapidly, violently, and with familiar consequences: borders redrawn, elites replaced, populations moved.

Out of Assyria's ruins rose the **Neo-Babylonian Empire**, often dated from **626 BCE**, when **Nabopolassar** rebelled against Assyrian domination, to **539 BCE**, when Babylon fell to the Persians. Neo-Babylon is remembered for its monumental city—the scale of its walls, its temples, its processional ways—and for a ruler whose campaigns left deep scars: **Nebuchadnezzar II** (reigned **605–562 BCE**). Under him, Babylon projected power westward; the kingdom of Judah was defeated, and **Jerusalem was destroyed in 587/586 BCE**, with many elites taken into exile. Babylon's empire was smaller than Assyria's peak, but it sat at the center of a region where memory and scripture would preserve its impact long after its armies were gone.

Yet even Babylon's grandeur sat inside the same Iron Age reality: mobility and logistics now shaped what states could attempt. Armies moved faster. Campaign seasons could stretch farther. Supply lines mattered more. A state that could organize transport, fodder, and storage could strike where an older palace system would have stalled. Then came the empire that turned these lessons into a template.

When **Cyrus II of Persia** began expanding in the mid-sixth century BCE—defeating the Medes (commonly dated around **550 BCE**) and taking **Babylon in 539 BCE**—he inherited a landscape full of battered cities, experienced administrators, and trade routes that still connected Asia to the Mediterranean. The **Achaemenid Empire** did not invent imperial rule from nothing. It absorbed existing practices and scaled them with unusual discipline. Its genius was not only conquest. It was governance across distance.

Under rulers like **Darius I** (reigned **522-486 BCE**), the empire organized territory into **satrapies**, provinces governed by officials responsible for tribute and order. The system varied by region and evolved over time, but the basic idea was consistent: rule locally through structured oversight, while keeping ultimate authority at the center. Persian kings presented themselves not merely as war leaders, but as guardians of order in a multi-ethnic realm. That claim could be pragmatic—tolerating local customs and religions where it served stability—while still extracting resources and demanding loyalty. And it ran on roads.

A courier rides hard along a packed track that cuts across dry hills toward a relay station. His horse is lathered. He does not stop to bargain for food; the station exists for him. A fresh mount is waiting. A small store of provisions is kept under guard. He exchanges a token of authority and is moving again within minutes.

This is the logic that later Greek observers admired in Persian communications: a relay system that made messages travel with a speed unimaginable in a purely local world. The most famous route, often called the **Royal Road**, linked major centers such as **Susa** and **Sardis**, tying the Iranian plateau to Anatolia. The details of route length and travel times vary depending on conditions, but the strategic effect is clear: an empire that can move information quickly can respond to rebellion, coordinate campaigns, and keep distant satraps from drifting into independence as easily.

Cavalry mattered here too, but not only in battle. Horses are fuel for empire—literally. They require fodder and care. An empire that fields large mounted forces must secure grazing lands, supply lines, and stable breeding. That demand ties military capacity to administrative reach. It is one reason Persian power, like Assyrian power before it, depended on controlling corridors rather than merely winning single fights.

So the Iron Age "new war systems" are not a single invention. They are a bundle: Iron spreads widely enough to make tools and weapons more locally accessible, reducing dependence on distant tin in a world where trade can be disrupted. Horses shift warfare away from purely elite chariot displays toward more flexible mounted systems—scouting, raiding, pursuit, rapid response. Siegecraft becomes professionalized, turning walled cities from near-invincible refuges into targets that can be reduced by method. Administration thickens, because feeding armies and keeping provinces loyal requires records, standards, and enforceable extraction. Roads and courier networks bind the whole together, making the empire feel present even in distant fields.

And in the shadows of all this motion, ordinary life adjusts again. A frontier farmer's anxieties change shape. He worries about raids, yes, but also about requisition orders—grain demanded for a passing army, animals taken for transport, labor summoned for road repair. He also benefits from the same system: markets that function, predictable measures, a reduction in the petty violence that often follows political fragmentation. Empire is never simply oppression or simply order. It is both, distributed unevenly.

By the time the Achaemenid template is in full stride, the Near East and eastern Mediterranean are no longer just a mosaic of cities and kingdoms. They are parts of a wider imperial ecology where power can travel fast, where logistics can sustain campaigns far from home, and where legitimacy has to be argued in universal terms—order, justice, divine favor—because a ruler is now addressing peoples with different gods and different memories. This leads directly to what comes next.

Because the bigger empires become, the more they need ideas that can bind strangers, justify rule, and answer the unease that grows when old certainties break. The Iron Age did not only create new weapons and faster roads. It created new moral questions—about kingship, justice, suffering, duty, and the self—that would soon be asked in new languages across a wide world.

The courier rides on, hoofbeats fading into heat shimmer, carrying orders that will move soldiers and grain and lives. Behind him, a siege ramp hardens in the sun, and a city waits for impact. Somewhere else, a merchant ship slips between islands with cargo that will outlast a king's campaign.

20

New Moral Worlds

The bowl is plain, darkened by use, smooth where countless fingers have gripped its rim. In the early light it catches no attention at all, which is part of its purpose. The man carrying it walks slowly along the edge of a village on the Ganges plain, not hurried, not begging in the desperate sense, but receiving what is offered—handfuls of rice, a ladle of lentils, a scrap of flatbread. The donors do not know his thoughts. He does not know theirs. Yet for a moment they are bound by a new kind of exchange: food for discipline, generosity for merit, the ordinary life of householders touching the renunciation of someone who has stepped out of it.

A few thousand kilometers away and a few decades in either direction depending on which tradition you follow, another young man sits cross-legged with bamboo slips spread like ribs across his lap. Each slip holds neat brushstrokes, tied into bundles that can be carried, copied, rearranged. He studies by lamplight, memorizing not only words but a way of standing in the world—how to treat elders, how to serve a ruler, how to govern himself so that others might follow.

Across the sea, in an Athenian courtyard scented with wine and olive oil, men recline on couches as a flute player's notes float through the heat. Cups pass. Arguments begin softly and then sharpen. What is justice? What is virtue? What does a good life look like if the gods do not speak clearly and the city's laws can be voted up or down by ordinary citizens with loud opinions and short tempers?

Three scenes. Three objects. A bowl, bamboo slips, a wine cup. None of them looks like an empire. Yet each belongs to an age shaped by empires, wars, and growing states—an age when the old answers, rooted in village custom and temple ritual, began to feel too small for the scale of human life.

Between roughly **800 and 200 BCE**—with different clocks in different regions—large parts of Eurasia experienced intense political competition and social change. Cities grew. Coinage and markets expanded in some places. Armies marched farther and more often. Taxation and debt reached deeper into households. Writing became more common as an administrative tool, even if literacy remained limited. People were uprooted by conquest and resettlement. The world felt wider and less predictable. When life expands in scale like that, the most urgent questions expand too.

Who has the right to rule? What do we owe each other? Why do good people suffer? What, exactly, is a self? If the old rituals keep working for the harvest but not for the heart, where do you look next?

What emerged was not one unified "Axial Age" awakening with a single timetable. It was a cluster of new moral worlds—religions and philosophies that redefined authority and the person, often by shifting weight from public sacrifice to inner discipline, from tribal gods to universal principles, from inherited status to ethical conduct. Some traditions still honored ritual. Some challenged it. Some gave rulers new legitimacy tools. Some armed critics of rulers. All of them changed the long-term vocabulary of human meaning.

Start with a tradition forged in a small kingdom caught between larger powers.

In the hills of the Levant, the kingdoms of **Israel** and **Judah** lived in the shadow of empires. Assyria's expansion in the eighth century BCE destroyed the northern kingdom of Israel (**722/721 BCE** in the conventional dating for the fall of Samaria), while Judah survived longer under pressure, tribute, and political danger. Then came Babylon. In the early sixth century BCE, Babylonian forces under **Nebuchadnezzar II** destroyed Jerusalem and its temple (**587/586 BCE**), and many elites were exiled.

Exile is not only a human tragedy. It is also an intellectual shock. If your religious life is tied to a temple and land, what happens when you lose both? One answer is to rebuild ritual elsewhere. Another is to turn memory into text, and identity into covenant.

Hebrew traditions already contained powerful ethical strands in prophetic critique: insistence that justice matters more than mere ceremony, that rulers are accountable, that oppression is not erased by offerings. Under the pressures of conquest, defeat, and displacement, these ideas hardened into something even more durable: a community defined not only by territory but by law, story, and a relationship with one God who claims universal authority. Monotheism here is not simply a theological statement; it is a moral and political one. If there is one supreme God, then no empire is sacred by nature. Kings can be judged. Nations can be humbled. History becomes a stage on which righteousness and betrayal matter.

When some exiles returned under Persian rule and the temple was rebuilt (traditionally **516 BCE** for the Second Temple's completion), the religion that emerged was not a return to an older simplicity. It was a tradition increasingly anchored in texts, interpretation, and communal practice that could survive displacement. A people with a portable law can endure what a temple alone cannot.

Now turn east to the Iranian world, where empire itself becomes a moral claim. The religion associated with **Zoroaster (Zarathustra)** is difficult to date precisely; scholars debate when he lived and how early the teachings took the form we later recognize. What is clearer is that by the time the **Achaemenid Persian** kings were building an empire in the sixth and fifth centuries BCE, royal inscriptions present their rule as aligned with **Ahura Mazda**, a supreme deity invoked as the source of legitimate kingship. In these inscriptions, the king fights not only enemies but "the Lie," presenting order as a moral struggle rather than mere dominance.

Zoroastrian thought, in its mature forms, emphasizes a cosmic contest between truth and deceit, order and chaos, and it frames human choices as consequential within that struggle. This is not morality as private feeling. It is morality as participation in the structure of reality. It also suits an empire that must rule diverse peoples: the king can claim legitimacy through alignment with a universal order rather than through the narrow god of a single city.

At the same time, the Iranian world sits on crossroads where ideas travel. Later Jewish and Christian traditions would develop strong themes of judgment, angels, and end times; how much of that reflects direct Zoroastrian influence remains debated, but the broader pattern is unmistakable. When empires expand, moral imaginaries expand too. The universe becomes more morally organized in thought because human society feels more organized and more dangerous in practice.

In northern India, the question took a different shape: not "Which empire is rightful?" but "What is the self, and why does life hurt?"

The older Vedic tradition centered on ritual expertise and sacrifice, performed by priests to sustain cosmic order and social hierarchy. But over time, especially across the **late second and early first millennium BCE**, new reflections emerged in texts later called the **Upanishads** (composed over centuries, roughly **800–300 BCE** in common scholarly ranges). These works do not abandon ritual so much as move behind it. They ask what sacrifice *means*. They probe the relationship between **atman** (self) and **brahman** (ultimate reality), and they develop ideas of **karma** and rebirth as moral causality stretching beyond one lifetime.

This is a profound reorientation. It suggests that the deepest truth is not only in public performance but in inward knowledge, and that liberation is possible through insight and discipline. In a world where social life was becoming more stratified and political power more competitive, the promise of an inner escape from the cycle of suffering held real force.

Out of that ferment came movements that challenged the authority of sacrifice more directly.

By the time we reach the lifetime traditionally associated with the **Buddha** (often placed in the **fifth century BCE**, though exact chronology is debated) and **Mahavira** (a key figure in **Jain** tradition, often placed around the **sixth–fifth centuries BCE**), the Gangetic plain was dotted with cities, states, merchants, and armies. Wealth could be accumulated. Debt could ruin. War could uproot entire regions. The old village gods and rituals did not always speak clearly to this new world.

Buddhism offered a diagnosis that did not require a creator god or a hereditary priesthood: life involves suffering; suffering has causes; causes can be understood; a path exists to end it. The path demanded ethical conduct, mental discipline, and wisdom, embodied in communities of renunciants who lived on alms—like the man with the begging bowl at dawn. This was radical in practice even when it was gentle in tone. It created an institution, the **sangha**, that could cross political boundaries. It offered moral authority independent of kings, while also being attractive to kings who wanted legitimacy through patronage and merit.

Jainism pushed renunciation even further, placing **ahimsa** (non-violence) at the center with a ferocity that could be socially disruptive and morally magnetic. In a world of animal sacrifice, warfare, and exploitation, the refusal to harm became a kind of moral weapon. It also shaped economic patterns: communities committed to non-violence often favored trades that avoided killing, and over time Jain merchant patronage became influential in many regions.

The point is not that everyone became a monk. Most people did not. The point is that these traditions offered new frameworks in which the self mattered, intention mattered, and moral truth could stand apart from birth and state.

In China, the pressure came from a different direction: not empire fully formed, but the grinding crisis of states that could not stop fighting.

During the **Spring and Autumn** and **Warring States** periods (traditionally dated from **770 to 221 BCE**), dozens of polities competed, reformed their armies, built bureaucracies, and turned war into a relentless fact of life. Old aristocratic rituals that once stabilized hierarchy began to feel hollow amid betrayal and slaughter. If society was breaking, what could bind it again?

Confucius (551–479 BCE) offered an answer rooted in human relationships and ritual reformed into ethics. He treated **li** (ritual propriety) not as empty ceremony but as a discipline that shapes character and social harmony. He emphasized **ren** (humaneness), filial devotion, and the moral responsibility of rulers. The ideal ruler in this vision does not govern mainly through punishment. He governs by example, making virtue contagious.

It was an answer suited to a world where violence had become normalized and governance desperately needed legitimacy beyond fear. Confucianism did not reject the state. It tried to civilize it.

Alongside it grew another current often gathered under the umbrella of **Daoism**, with foundational texts like the **Daodejing** (its dating debated, commonly placed somewhere in the late Zhou era) and later works like the **Zhuangzi** (often associated with the fourth–third centuries BCE). Daoist thought questioned the frantic human urge to control and categorize. It praised alignment with the **Dao**—the Way—through simplicity, humility, and **wu wei**, a kind of non-forcing action. Where Confucianism tried to repair society through cultivated virtue and correct relationships, Daoism often suggested that society's very striving creates the sickness it wants to cure. In times of war and heavy administration, that counter-voice matters. It offers refuge, critique, and a different ideal of freedom.

Now cross again to the Greek world, where small city-states produced questions that would travel far beyond their size. In Greece from the sixth century BCE onward, thinkers later called **pre-Socratics** began asking what the world is made of, seeking principles beneath myth. But it is in classical Athens of the fifth and fourth centuries BCE that philosophy becomes a social practice: debate in public spaces, argument as a craft, skepticism toward easy authority. Democracy, lawsuits, factional politics, and imperial ambition forced Athenians to confront uncomfortable realities: the crowd can be wrong, rhetoric can overpower truth, and the city's glory can ride on violence done elsewhere.

In that setting, **Socrates** became famous not for writing but for questioning. He asked what people meant by virtue, justice, piety—then showed how quickly confident answers collapsed under scrutiny. His execution in **399 BCE** for impiety and corrupting the youth became a warning: even a city that prides itself on freedom can punish those who challenge its moral foundations.

After him, **Plato** and **Aristotle** built systems that treated ethics and politics as fields of inquiry rather than inherited custom. Greek philosophy did not merely compete with religion; it offered another kind of authority: reasoned argument, observation, and the pursuit of definitions that could hold across cases. It also produced a new kind of selfhood: a person responsible not only to gods and city, but to an internal standard of rational consistency.

Return to the symposium scene. The wine loosens tongues, but the best arguments do not come from looseness. They come from discipline: the ability to follow a thought to its end, to accept that you might be wrong, to live under questions without flinching. In a world where states could demand obedience, that mental independence had political implications whether philosophers intended it or not.

So what links these "new moral worlds" across so many regions?

Not a shared doctrine. They disagreed on almost everything: gods or no gods, ritual central or suspect, salvation personal or social, reason supreme or limited. The common thread is pressure and scale. As societies grew more complex and power reached deeper into life, people needed moral languages that could address strangers, institutions, and suffering that was no longer explained by a bad harvest alone. They developed ethics that could travel: commandments, virtues, paths, principles. They developed authority sources that could rival mere force: sacred law, cosmic truth, inner enlightenment, rational argument, ancestral mandate.

And once such languages exist, rulers cannot ignore them. They can patronize them, borrow from them, or persecute them. Either way, the relationship between power and meaning changes. Legitimacy becomes something you can debate, not merely inherit.

The man with the begging bowl completes his morning circuit and returns to a shaded place to eat quietly. The food is simple. The discipline is the point. Nearby, householders return to their work, still tied to fields and taxes and family obligations, but now living in a world where a different kind of authority has appeared: the authority of a path, a text, a virtue, a conscience.

In China, the student ties his bamboo slips together and stands, carrying his learning like a burden and a weapon. In Athens, the symposium ends, and arguments linger into the next day like a hangover of ideas. These moral worlds will not stay local. Conquest, trade, and empire will carry them outward, and they will reshape politics as much as they reshape souls.

21

City Pride to Empire Dreams

Bronze scrapes against bronze as the line tightens. A man shifts the weight of his shield—wood faced with metal, heavy enough to bite into his forearm—and feels the press of another shield against his left side. The helmet narrows his world to breath and glare. Ahead, the ground is flat and dusty, and beyond it another line is doing the same silent preparation. Someone calls a cadence. Feet stamp. Spears lower. For a moment everything is contained: fear, pride, discipline, the simple fact that if you break formation you die.

This is a hoplite's war, the kind that belongs to a particular political invention: the **polis**, the Greek city-state. In the polis, the citizen is not merely a subject. He is, at least in theory, a participant in rule and a bearer of duty. He pays, he argues, he votes, he fights. His armor is partly his own expense, which means war is tied to property and status. His place in the line reflects his place in the city. The formation is a political diagram drawn in sweat.

Yet this world of small states, proud and quarrelsome, sits on the edge of something much larger. Beyond the Aegean lies the vast imperial system built by the Persians, and beyond that, routes that reach into Asia. Greek history cannot be told as a purely European story. From the beginning, it is a frontier story—small polities negotiating with empires, borrowing from them, fearing them, resisting them, imitating them, and eventually, under one Macedonian king, inheriting their scale.

The polis is where the Greek story begins in its distinctive form. From roughly the **eighth to the fifth centuries BCE**, Greek communities across the Aegean and beyond organized into city-states with their own laws, cults, and political experiments. Some were oligarchies dominated by aristocratic families. Some developed forms of broader participation. **Athens**, especially, turned into a laboratory of politics in the late sixth and fifth centuries BCE, with reforms that expanded citizen involvement (while excluding women, enslaved people, and resident foreigners). **Sparta**, in a different direction, built a militarized society that subordinated individual life to state discipline and maintained its citizen body through the exploitation of the helot population.

The polis world was competitive by nature. With many small states crowded into a landscape of limited arable land, rivalry was constant—over borders, trade, prestige, and control of sanctuaries. Colonization spread Greek-speaking communities around the Mediterranean and Black Sea from the eighth century BCE onward, creating networks of exchange and identity that expanded the Greek world far beyond mainland Greece. But expansion did not create unity. It created more points of contact, more rivalries, more opportunities.

Then the Persian Empire brought the question of scale into the Greek imagination. By the early fifth century BCE, tensions between Persian rule and Greek cities in Anatolia contributed to conflict that pulled mainland Greek states into a wider war. The traditional timeline is familiar: the Persian expedition under Darius I ends with the battle of **Marathon (490 BCE)**; the larger invasion under Xerxes includes **Thermopylae** and **Salamis (480 BCE)** and **Plataea (479 BCE)**. Each battle has been mythologized, often flattened into a simple tale of "East versus West." The reality is more tangled. Greek states were divided, some collaborated, and Persian imperial policy was complex rather than purely tyrannical. But the wars mattered because they fused Greek identity into a sharper, if still contested, sense of "we," defined partly by resistance to empire. Resistance brought consequences.

Athens emerged from the Persian Wars with prestige and a powerful navy. It led, and increasingly dominated, the **Delian League**, a coalition that began as a defensive alliance but evolved into an Athenian empire in practice, extracting tribute and enforcing compliance. Sparta and its allies saw this as a threat. The result was the long, bitter **Peloponnesian War (431–404 BCE)**, which Thucydides recorded with a cold eye for fear, ambition, and the corrosion of moral language under pressure. The war weakened the Greek world and exposed the limits of polis competition: small states could fight each other until they were exhausted, leaving openings for powers with deeper resources. That opening widened from the north.

Macedon, long treated by many southern Greeks as semi-outsider, was transformed under **Philip II** (reigned **359–336 BCE**) into a formidable military state. Philip reorganized the army, famously strengthening the phalanx with long spears (sarissas) and integrating cavalry and tactical flexibility. He exploited Greek divisions and defeated a coalition of Greek city-states at **Chaeronea (338 BCE)**, establishing Macedonian dominance. The polis system did not vanish, but its freedom narrowed. The stage was set for Philip's son to aim beyond Greece entirely.

That son was **Alexander III**, remembered as Alexander the Great. In **334 BCE**, Alexander crossed into Asia and began a campaign that would dismantle the Achaemenid Persian Empire within a decade. The headlines are dramatic—**Granicus**, **Issus (333 BCE)**, **Gaugamela (331 BCE)**—but the deeper significance lies in what conquest did to the Mediterranean and Near Eastern world. Alexander's march connected Greece, Egypt, Mesopotamia, Iran, and parts of Central and South Asia under a single moving center of power. He took **Egypt** and founded a city that would become symbolic of the new age: **Alexandria**. He entered Babylon. He pursued Persian king Darius III until the old imperial order fractured beyond repair.

Alexander did not simply destroy. He also absorbed. He adopted elements of Persian court practice, took on titles that signaled universal kingship, and attempted to bind Macedonian and Persian elites through marriages and shared service. These policies created resentment among some of his Macedonian followers, who feared the loss of their status and identity. Alexander's empire was held together by charisma, speed, and constant campaigning. It lacked a stable succession plan. When he died in **323 BCE** in Babylon, still young, the world he had torn open did what worlds do when a central force vanishes: it fractured and reformed.

The **Hellenistic** age begins in that aftermath. Alexander's generals—later called the **Diadochi**—fought for control of different parts of the empire. Over time, several major successor kingdoms stabilized, including the **Ptolemaic** dynasty in Egypt, the **Seleucid** empire across much of the Near East, and the **Antigonid** kingdom in Macedonia. Borders shifted repeatedly. Wars were frequent. Yet the shared cultural effects of Alexander's conquests endured beyond any single battle line.

"Hellenistic" does not mean "Greek replaces everything." It means blending at scale. Greek became a widely used language of administration and elite culture in many regions, but it coexisted with local languages and traditions. Cities were founded or refounded, often with Greek-style institutions, theaters, and gymnasia, but they sat on older sacred landscapes and older economies. Rulers presented themselves with Greek titles and iconography while also honoring local gods to secure legitimacy. A temple in Egypt could still look Egyptian even under Greek-speaking kings. A city in Syria could host Greek-style civic life while living amid Semitic religious traditions. The world became more mixed, not more uniform.

To feel this, walk into a port. A merchant stands on a quay where the smell of fish, oil, and wet wood mixes with incense smoke. He hears languages overlap—Greek shouted by sailors, Aramaic in bargaining, Egyptian spoken by dock workers, perhaps Persian or other tongues carried by travelers. He handles coins stamped with a ruler's face, yet he also negotiates by weight and trust as merchants always have. His cargo might include grain from the Nile, wine from the Aegean, papyrus, glass, spices or aromatics moving through longer routes. He is not thinking about "Hellenism." He is thinking about margins, risks, and whether the next ship arrives on time. But his life depends on a world that conquest has connected.

The Hellenistic kingdoms competed fiercely, but they also invested in cities as engines of wealth and legitimacy. Urban life expanded. Markets deepened. Armies required funding and supply. Bureaucracies grew. And the cosmopolitan city became a new kind of social stage where identity could be flexible. A person might be "Greek" by language and education but local by religion and family ties. A Jewish community in Alexandria could translate sacred texts into Greek while maintaining its own law and tradition. A Syrian or Egyptian elite could adopt Greek learning as a tool of status without abandoning older loyalties.

This is also the age when science and scholarship gain institutional homes on an unprecedented scale. In Alexandria, under the Ptolemies, royal patronage helped build centers of learning associated with the **Library** and the **Mouseion**. The details of the library's size and organization are debated, and much is wrapped in later legend, but what matters is the ambition: to gather texts, to classify knowledge, to host scholars whose work served prestige and statecraft. Knowledge became an imperial asset.

Picture an Alexandrian librarian—more accurately, a scholar within that institutional world—unrolling a papyrus scroll under steady light. He checks a catalog, compares copies, argues over the correct line of a poem, or calculates the geometry of a shadow. In this city, scholarship is not only private curiosity. It is part of a court's claim to universal importance. Rulers want to be patrons of learning because learning confers legitimacy and attracts talent.

From this scholarly ecosystem came work that later generations would treat as foundations: **Euclid's** geometry, **Eratosthenes** estimating the Earth's circumference, advances in astronomy, engineering, medicine, and mechanics. None of this was purely Greek invention detached from the wider world. The Hellenistic age sat at crossroads where Babylonian astronomical traditions, Egyptian administrative knowledge, and many local practices intersected with Greek mathematical argumentation. The mixed world produced mixed knowledge. And yet, the polis did not entirely die. It changed.

Greek city-states continued to exist, to argue, to fight, to form leagues. Civic identity remained potent. Even under kings, many cities retained local councils and assemblies, and citizens continued to think in terms of civic honor and autonomy. The Hellenistic kings needed cities; cities negotiated with kings. The political vocabulary of the polis—citizenship, law, public debate—continued to shape the Mediterranean imagination.

Competition inside Greece forged political experimentation and intense cultural life. Conflict with Persia sharpened identity and revealed the stakes of empire. Macedon exploited Greek division, and Alexander tore open a continent-spanning space. The successor kingdoms stabilized the chaos enough to build new cities, new bureaucracies, and new cultural fusions. In these cities, learning and trade flourished, and the Mediterranean became more connected in daily practice than ever before.

But connection brings new tensions. Empires demand taxes. Armies demand grain. Kings demand loyalty. Cities demand autonomy. Cultural blending can be creative, but it can also produce backlash. The Hellenistic world is full of revolts, succession crises, and regions that resist being absorbed into a king's map. And beyond the Greek-speaking zones, other powers are rising with their own political languages and ambitions.

Return to the hoplite from the opening scene. The old citizen-soldier ideal is still spoken of, still honored in stories, but the Mediterranean around him has changed. Wars are no longer only seasonal clashes between neighboring cities. They are campaigns of kings with professional armies and vast supply needs. The decisions that shape his life might be made in a palace far away, in a court where Greek is spoken with many accents.

In Alexandria, the scholar sets down a scroll and reaches for another, surrounded by shelves that represent a new dream: that knowledge can be gathered, ordered, and made universal. On the dock, the merchant watches a ship ease into harbor, its sails slackening, its hull heavy with goods and the invisible weight of connection. The polis world produced fierce independence and intense rivalry. The Hellenistic world produced mixture, scale, and new forms of power.

22

Empire on the Trade Wind

The stone is cool under the morning sun, as if it has kept a little night inside it. A pillar rises from the ground with a steadiness that makes nearby trees look temporary. Its surface is polished to a soft sheen, not quite reflective, but smooth enough that rain slides off cleanly. Letters run down it in careful lines. They are not the curling, decorative marks of a temple blessing. They read like a public notice meant to be understood by people who will never meet the man who ordered them carved.

It is the voice of a king speaking beyond his lifetime. It does not boast of a palace. It does not list conquered cities like trophies. It insists on something stranger: restraint, fairness, compassion, discipline. It tells officials how to behave. It tells subjects what is expected and what is promised. It tells the world that power can justify itself in moral terms, not only in military ones.

To understand how such a pillar could stand in the middle of South Asia, you have to begin a few centuries earlier, when the subcontinent's political landscape was not one empire but many rival kingdoms and republics, each testing how large a state could become, and what kind of life it could demand from the people beneath it.

By roughly the **sixth century BCE**, northern India's Gangetic plain was thick with new settlements and growing towns. Iron tools, spreading across the region over time, made clearing forest and working heavy soils more feasible. Wet-rice agriculture and intensified farming supported larger populations. Trade routes deepened, tying river valleys to foothills, forests, and distant coasts. Money, in the form of **punch-marked coins**, began to circulate in many areas, making taxes, wages, and market exchange easier to standardize. The world was becoming denser and more connected, and politics responded the way it often does when density rises: through competition, consolidation, and institutional experimentation.

Later texts remember this era as the time of the **Mahajanapadas**, the "great realms," commonly enumerated as sixteen. Lists vary, but the rough shape is consistent: major polities like **Magadha**, **Kosala**, **Avanti**, **Vatsa**, and others jostled for advantage, while some regions experimented with oligarchic or republican forms often described as **gana-sanghas**. The point is not the exact list. The point is the scale. These were not small chiefdoms. They were states with armies, taxes, diplomacy, and ambitions.

If you were a traveler in this period, you would have felt the new pressure of borders. There were officials at gates. There were tolls at crossings. There were rules about weights and measures, and punishments for breaking them. There were monasteries and markets rising alongside fortifications. There were roads crowded with carts and foot travelers, and in roadside rest houses the talk was not only of harvests and marriages, but of kings and wars, and which realm was expanding this season.

And in the middle of that competition, **Magadha**, in the lower Gangetic region, began to pull ahead. Its geography mattered. River networks supported transport and agriculture. Its rulers built resources and alliances. Over time, Magadhan power became the spine of a larger unification effort. This is the political soil out of which the **Maurya** empire would grow.

The Maurya story begins not as a peaceful merging of states, but as a hard consolidation in a world already shaped by empire. After Alexander's campaigns had cracked open the northwest and left behind successor politics and new military realities, the subcontinent's frontier zones were in flux. Into this moment stepped **Chandragupta Maurya**, usually dated to have come to power around **321 BCE**, establishing a new ruling house with its capital at **Pataliputra** (near modern Patna), a strategic city on the Ganges.

Pataliputra was not chosen by accident. It sat at a river junction that made it a natural administrative hub, able to pull resources from the countryside and push orders outward. The Mauryan state built power through what states always build it through: extraction, organization, and force made reliable.

You can see the state in motion in the figure of a caravan leader. He walks at the front, not because he is the strongest fighter, but because he knows the route. His animals are loaded with bundles: salt, cloth, metal goods, perhaps spices or aromatics depending on region and season. He carries documents or tokens that signal permission to travel, and he carries something less official that matters just as much: relationships. Which local chief can be bribed. Which village headman will offer shelter. Which garrison commander demands a toll beyond what the law allows. Which stretch of road invites bandits.

Under a strong empire, the promise is simple. Travel becomes safer. Routes become more predictable. Markets become larger because more people trust that goods will arrive. Under a strong empire, the caravan leader's world expands.

But the empire's promise has a cost. The same road that helps merchants also helps tax collectors and marching troops. The same safety that reduces banditry can increase surveillance. The same standardization that makes trade smoother can make evasion harder when the harvest is thin.

Mauryan administration, as far as we can reconstruct it from later texts and inscriptions, seems to have been substantial for its time: a central court, provincial divisions, officials responsible for revenue and order, and a state interest in information. The famous political treatise often called the **Arthashastra**, traditionally associated with **Kautilya (Chanakya)**, is difficult to date precisely in its final form, and it likely reflects layers compiled over time. Still, it preserves a picture of statecraft that fits the broader Mauryan reality: a state concerned with revenue, espionage, regulation, and the practical mechanics of holding a large territory together.

The Mauryas also held a reputation for military scale. Whether every number later reported is reliable is another matter, but the principle is sound: the empire maintained forces large enough to deter rivals and enforce authority across distance. Holding a subcontinent-sized realm was not a matter of one decisive battle. It was a matter of repeating presence: garrisons, roads, collectors, judges, and the unglamorous daily work of making orders stick.

Then, under Chandragupta's successors, the empire deepened. **Bindusara** (often dated **c. 297–268 BCE**) maintained the structure and extended influence. But it is his son who shifts the moral tone of the state so dramatically that a new voice enters the historical record with unusual clarity.

Ashoka, who ruled roughly **268–232 BCE**, is known not only because he was powerful, but because he left behind a public archive in stone:

his **edicts**, carved on rocks and pillars across a wide geography. They are among the most direct royal voices of the ancient world, and they reveal something both political and intimate: an attempt to govern by ethics as well as by force.

The turning point often named is the **Kalinga War**, commonly dated around **261 BCE**, fought in eastern India near the coast. Kalinga mattered because it controlled strategic corridors and maritime access. Conquest there was not simply territorial expansion. It was control of a hinge between inland power and ocean routes. The war was brutal, and in Ashoka's own account, its human cost became the event that forced a rethinking.

Ashoka does not claim that warfare is glorious. He describes remorse. He speaks of suffering inflicted and the moral weight of it. Then he makes a political move that is rare in ancient imperial rhetoric: he announces a new standard for governance, called **dhamma** in his inscriptions.

Dhamma is not a simple synonym for Buddhism, even if Ashoka was a Buddhist patron and personally committed. In the edicts, dhamma is a public ethic: respect for elders, kindness to servants and dependents, moderation, generosity, truthfulness, tolerance among religious communities. It includes practical governance measures too: welfare concerns, medical facilities for people and animals in some accounts, the appointment of officials to promote dhamma, and the insistence that justice and fair treatment matter.

This was not a rejection of the state's coercive capacity. The Mauryan machinery did not dissolve into kindness. Taxes were still collected. Officials still enforced. The empire still held power. But Ashoka tried to shift the justification of that power. Not merely, "I conquered." Not merely, "The gods chose me." Instead, "My rule should reduce suffering, and my officials should behave as if the governed are human beings, not just revenue."

That is why the pillar matters. A pillar is durable, visible, public. It puts ethics into the landscape as a constant reminder, not only to subjects but to the king's own administrators. It turns moral instruction into infrastructure.

Ashoka's dhamma also aimed outward. His edicts mention diplomatic outreach beyond India's borders, including references to Hellenistic rulers by name in some inscriptions. Whether every mission achieved its intended effect is less important than the ambition: the Mauryan state imagined itself as part of a wider world where ideas could travel alongside goods.

In Ashoka's time, trade did not pause for imperial virtue. It expanded, and it needed institutions. This is where **urban guilds**, often called **shrenis**, become visible as crucial actors. Guilds organized craftsmen and merchants: weavers, metalworkers, potters, ivory carvers, traders. They maintained standards, controlled training, pooled resources, and in some cases functioned almost like corporations, able to make loans, fund projects, and sponsor religious and civic works. When you see inscriptions at stupas and monasteries listing donors, you often see guilds as collective patrons, proof that economic organization was becoming a social force.

A guild is more than a business group. It is a way to stabilize trust in a large market. If a traveler buys cloth in one city and knows it came from a respected guild, the risk of fraud drops. If a ruler wants to tax trade without killing it, guilds can become negotiating partners. If a religious institution wants durable patronage, guilds can provide it. In a world of growing towns and longer routes, guilds are the connective tissue between household production and imperial-scale commerce.

After Ashoka, the Mauryan empire did not last indefinitely. By roughly **185 BCE**, the dynasty ended, and the subcontinent entered a period of **post-Mauryan** political reconfiguration. This was not simply "collapse" in the Bronze Age sense, with palaces burning and systems disappearing. Many institutions persisted. Cities remained. Trade continued. But unity fractured into multiple powers: regional kingdoms, new dynasties, and frontier polities shaped by Central Asian movements and Hellenistic legacies in the northwest. This fragmentation did not weaken connection. In some ways, it intensified it.

Without a single empire monopolizing power, merchant networks and port cities could become even more important, negotiating with multiple rulers, paying multiple tariffs, and building influence through wealth and credit. Overland routes linking India to Central Asia and beyond remained active, and maritime routes became ever more significant as knowledge of **monsoon winds** made Indian Ocean sailing more predictable for those who understood the seasonal rhythm.

That rhythm brings us to the port customs scene. At a coastal harbor, the air is sharp with salt and fish. The dock is crowded with shapes that belong to trade: amphora-like jars, bales of cloth, heaps of pepper or other spices depending on region and era, bundles of timber, stacks of beads. Sailors haul rope and curse at stubborn knots. Porters move like ants under loads. In the shade of an awning sits a customs official with scales and standardized weights. He is not a philosopher. He is an agent of the state, or of a local ruler, or of a port authority backed by merchants. His job is to turn movement into revenue.

He inspects the cargo. He assesses dues. He records quantities. A dispute breaks out over a measure, and a guild representative steps in, not with a sword but with credibility. If the official is corrupt, the merchant will complain to someone powerful. If the merchant cheats, the official can seize goods. The port is a place where law and commerce touch each other every minute.

This scene is the subcontinent's wider arc made visible. The Mauryan period showed how statecraft could scale across land corridors, using roads, officials, and extraction. The post-Mauryan world showed how commerce could thrive through plural power, with cities and guilds acting as stabilizers even when political authority was divided. It also showed how ethics and religion traveled with trade.

Buddhism, already strengthened by patronage and monastic networks, moved along routes and ports, offering merchants a moral vocabulary and institutions that provided lodging, trust, and social ties across distance. Other traditions did the same in their own ways. Trade does not only move goods. It moves habits, stories, and forms of community that make strangers less strange. So it is not simply that India built empires, then traded. It is that empire and trade were part of the same loop.

Competition among Mahajanapadas drove state formation and urban growth. The Mauryas unified much of the subcontinent and built administrative capacity that could protect and tax movement, making large-scale commerce more predictable. Ashoka introduced an imperial moral language that sought to discipline power, giving legitimacy a new tone without erasing coercion. After the Mauryan center weakened, regional powers multiplied, but the commercial and institutional infrastructure remained strong enough that trade and urban guilds continued to knit South Asia into wider networks, including ocean routes that would become even more important in the centuries ahead.

Return, finally, to the pillar. The letters remain while the man who ordered them is long gone. Dust settles into the carved grooves and rain washes it out again. People pass by without reading, or reading only parts, or reading and disagreeing with what it asks of them. That, too, is part of the point. A moral world is never simply adopted. It is argued with, practiced unevenly, used by rulers, used against rulers.

Somewhere inland, a caravan leader steps onto a road that has been walked for generations, calculating risks that change as dynasties rise and fall. Somewhere on the coast, a customs officer weighs a cargo while a merchant watches his hands closely. Somewhere a guild meets to settle a dispute and decide how to respond to a new tax. South Asia is not only a story of kings. It is a story of routes, institutions, and ethics traveling together.

23

The Blueprint of Rule

The man on the embankment is young enough that his face still holds softness, but his hands do not. They are split at the fingertips, dark with mud and lime, the nails broken down to rough crescents. He lifts a basket of packed earth onto his shoulder and climbs a ramp that disappears into dust. Around him, hundreds do the same. The work has a rhythm, like waves: step, breathe, heave, dump. Step again.

No one calls this place a "Great Wall" yet. It is a line of urgency—mounds and palisades, stone and tamped soil—stitched across ridges and passes where riders can appear without warning.

Supervisors count bodies. Scribes count baskets. A whip cracks somewhere behind the line, not every minute, but often enough that the sound becomes part of the landscape.

When the basket empties, the man's shoulders keep feeling its weight. He turns back down the ramp, blinking against the grit, and he understands something without having words for it: the state has become heavier than any single person. It can move him like a tool. It can move mountains of earth by moving thousands of men.

This is how China's first unification feels at ground level—not as a map with neat borders, but as conscript labor, measurable, punishable, repeatable. The Qin did not invent harshness, and they did not invent administration. What they did was fuse them into a system so tight that it could swallow rival kingdoms in a generation—and then, when it cracked, leave behind habits of rule that a new dynasty could inherit.

To see why unification became possible, you have to start in the centuries before it, when China was not one country but many, locked in a competition that turned governance into an arms race.

From roughly the **fifth century BCE** onward, during what later historians call the **Warring States** period (often dated **475–221 BCE**), polities fought with a scale and intensity that made older aristocratic orders look obsolete. Armies grew larger, more disciplined. Fortifications multiplied. Fields were surveyed and taxed more systematically. Bureaucracies thickened because war required predictable revenue, and predictable revenue required predictable control of people.

In that struggle, ideas about ruling sharpened. Some thinkers argued that morality and ritual should restore harmony. Others—often grouped under the label **Legalist**—argued something colder: good intentions are unreliable; human behavior can be shaped by clear laws, consistent rewards, and harsh punishments. If you want a state that survives, you do not rely on virtue. You build a machine.

No state embraced this logic more thoroughly than **Qin**, a western kingdom that spent generations reorganizing itself for conquest. Reforms associated with figures like **Shang Yang** in the **fourth century BCE** strengthened Qin by weakening hereditary privilege, rewarding military merit, standardizing administration, and tightening legal control. Qin became efficient in the way a sharpened blade is efficient: it does not need to be loved to cut.

By **221 BCE**, Qin's king had defeated the last rival and declared himself **Qin Shi Huang**, the "First Emperor." The title itself was a claim that history had turned a corner. Kings had existed for centuries. An emperor suggested something new: rule that stood above regional lineages and local traditions, rule that could be universal.

Unification is often told as a triumph of military genius. It was that, in part. But military victory alone cannot hold a continent-sized realm. The deeper Qin achievement—and the reason later dynasties could not simply return to a patchwork—was administrative.

The Qin moved fast to break the power of old aristocracies and regional identities. They replaced many hereditary structures with a system of **commandery and county** administration, staffed by appointed officials rather than local lords with their own independent bases of power. The goal was straightforward: loyalty flows upward to the center, not sideways to local strongmen.

Then came standardization, the quiet revolution that makes a conquered world governable. Weights and measures were unified so that taxes and trade could be assessed consistently. Coinage was standardized so that payments and state purchases could be made without endless conversion. Axle widths, road gauges, and written forms were brought into closer alignment, not because uniformity is beautiful, but because it reduces friction. A cart that fits the road, a document that can be read in the next province, a measure that means the same thing in two markets—these are the small hinges on which a large state swings.

Even writing became part of this program. The Qin promoted a standardized script style often associated with **small seal script**, helping officials communicate across regions with different local traditions. The motive was not cultural purity. It was control. If the center can read what the periphery writes, it can govern it.

Control also meant surveillance over thought, or at least over the institutions that transmit thought. The Qin are infamous for measures aimed at suppressing dissenting texts and traditions—later remembered as "burning books and burying scholars," with details that historians continue to scrutinize carefully. What matters for our purposes is not the sensational image but the political impulse behind it: a state trying to prevent alternative authority—from old aristocratic memory, from rival philosophies, from regional loyalties—from undermining a newly unified center. And all of this ran on labor.

The wall lines in the north, the roads and canals, the palaces and the First Emperor's mausoleum complex—these projects required immense mobilization. Conscript labor was not a side effect of Qin rule. It was the fuel. People were registered. Households were assigned obligations. Officials supervised quotas. Punishments enforced compliance. You could call this the cost of unification, paid in blistered hands and shortened lives. It worked—until it didn't.

The Qin empire was astonishingly fast in conquest and terrifyingly brittle in legitimacy. The same harshness that made it efficient also made it hated. When Qin Shi Huang died in **210 BCE**, succession struggles and court politics weakened the center at the worst possible moment. Revolts erupted. Within a few years, the Qin state collapsed, and by **206 BCE** the dynasty was gone.

If you stop the story there, you might think the Qin were a failed experiment, a nightmare that burned out. But history's deeper pattern is different. The Qin did not leave a lasting dynasty, but they left a lasting *structure*. They proved unification could be done, and they left behind tools—administrative divisions, standardization habits, legal procedures, centralized registers—that a successor could pick up and use with a steadier hand.

That successor was the **Han**. In **202 BCE**, after years of conflict, **Liu Bang**—a man of relatively humble origins compared to many aristocratic rivals—emerged as emperor, known as **Han Gaozu**. The Han inherited a landscape exhausted by war but already reshaped by Qin centralization. Their challenge was not to reinvent rule from nothing. It was to keep the machinery running without snapping the people.

Han consolidation was, in many ways, a negotiation with the Qin legacy. The Han kept much of the centralized administrative framework, because it worked. They continued governing through appointed officials and territorial divisions that allowed the center to monitor provinces. They maintained standardized systems that made revenue predictable. But they softened the most brutal edges when they could, balancing law with a broader legitimacy story.

This is where ideology returns—not as philosophy in a scholar's room, but as a tool of statecraft. Over time, especially under **Emperor Wu** (reigned **141–87 BCE**), the Han increasingly promoted **Confucian** moral language as a public ideal, even as Legalist administrative techniques remained embedded in practice. The state could demand obedience through law, but it could also present itself as guardian of order and morality, with the emperor as a Son of Heaven responsible for harmony. This blend—hard administration wrapped in moral legitimacy—became one of the most durable political formulas in world history.

Durable, however, does not mean gentle. The Han state still needed revenue. It still needed soldiers. It still needed control over the countryside. That reality becomes visible in a different scene: the market.

A market inspector walks through a crowded street in a walled city—**Chang'an**, perhaps, in the early Han world—where stalls spill over with cloth, grain, tools, lacquerware, salt, and meat. The inspector carries standardized weights and a seal of authority. He checks measures, tests scales, enforces rules on prices or permitted goods depending on policy and period. He is not a philosopher, and he is not a soldier, but he is one of the state's most intimate faces: the person who makes the abstract idea of standardization real.

To the seller who tries to shave a measure, he is a threat. To the buyer tired of fraud, he is protection. To the state, he is a revenue safeguard. His work is small and constant, and that is exactly why it matters. Empires are held not only by armies but by routines that make daily life legible to authority.

Beyond the cities, the Han faced a problem that defined their foreign policy: the **Xiongnu**. To the north, across the steppe, powerful nomadic confederations could move faster than any settled army and strike where walls were thin. The Xiongnu were not a single tribe with a single leader forever; they were a shifting political confederation capable of coordinating raids and diplomacy across vast grasslands. They were dangerous precisely because they were mobile and hard to pin down.

The early Han, still consolidating after civil war, often sought accommodation through policies known as **heqin**—marriage alliances and gift exchanges intended to buy peace. Such arrangements were not simple "appeasement." They were diplomacy under constraint, a recognition that constant war was unaffordable while the dynasty was still stabilizing.

But accommodation had limits. Border raids continued. The drain on resources and prestige grew. Under Emperor Wu, the Han shifted toward aggressive campaigns aimed at breaking Xiongnu power and reshaping the northern frontier. War on the steppe was not like war between walled cities. It demanded horses, fodder, supply lines stretched across harsh terrain, and commanders capable of operating at long distances.

This is where the border envoy comes into view. In **138 BCE**, Emperor Wu sent an envoy named **Zhang Qian** westward, seeking alliances and intelligence that might help counter the Xiongnu. Zhang Qian's journey is remembered partly because it was dramatic—captivity, long detours, difficult returns—and partly because it revealed something strategic: beyond the steppe and deserts lay a chain of peoples, states, and markets in Central Asia. The Han were not alone on the edge of the world. They were neighbors to a wider Eurasian web.

Out of such missions, and out of the military push into frontier corridors, the routes later called the **Silk Road** began to take more recognizable shape. "Silk Road" is a modern label, and it can mislead by suggesting a single highway. In reality it was a network: oasis towns, mountain passes, caravan routes, and diplomatic corridors connecting China to Central Asia and, indirectly, to the Mediterranean world.

Silk mattered because it was light, valuable, and desirable in foreign courts. But silk did not travel alone. Neither did ideas. Horses came east; precious stones, glass, and metal goods moved; religious and cultural influences would later follow more strongly. The Silk Road was not merely a commercial invention. It was an imperial byproduct. To fight the Xiongnu and secure the frontier, the Han pushed into the west. To sustain that push, they needed alliances and supply. Those needs opened routes. Routes created markets. Markets created new interests that wanted stability. Empire and exchange fed each other.

Technology was the quiet partner in all of this, shaping what the state could demand and what it could deliver.

Iron tools expanded agricultural productivity and made clearing and cultivation more feasible in many regions, increasing the taxable surplus that could support armies and officials. The Han period is also associated with sophisticated use of crossbows and improvements in metallurgy and manufacturing that supported mass provisioning of forces. Standardized production and state-controlled workshops in some contexts allowed the government to equip troops more predictably than a purely local system could. Even the mundane technologies of record-keeping—seals, registers, standardized documents—were forms of power. They turned people into entries in a system: taxable, conscriptable, punishable, protectable.

And there is always the human cost again, returning like a refrain. A conscript on a frontier road does not care whether the state calls itself moral. He cares whether his family eats while he is away. He cares whether he returns. He learns quickly that unification means the state can reach him in a village his grandfather barely left. He learns that law is not an abstract principle but an official with a tally. He learns that ideology can be a comfort and a threat: a language that says the empire is order, and therefore resistance is chaos.

Yet many also learned the opposite lesson: that a strong state can make life more predictable. It can suppress banditry. It can standardize markets. It can build infrastructure that makes famine less catastrophic in some regions and periods. It can create avenues for talent to rise through service, at least for some classes, because administration needs capable people. The Han state was not a simple villain. It was a vast bargain, unevenly distributed.

That bargain is why the Qin–Han story matters far beyond China. Qin unification demonstrated that law, standardization, and centralized administration could replace a fractured landscape of competing states. Han consolidation demonstrated that the same machinery could be stabilized by blending coercion with legitimacy, and by turning bureaucracy into a long-term system rather than a short-lived conquest tool. The frontier wars and diplomacy with the Xiongnu forced the Han to think beyond the agricultural heartland, opening corridors that would connect Eurasia more tightly over centuries. Markets, inspectors, envoys, soldiers—these were the people who made the empire real.

Return to the market inspector in the city street. He stops at a stall and lifts a weight, tests it, watches the seller's eyes. A small correction is made, a fine threatened or imposed. The crowd moves on. The day continues. Nothing about this moment looks like a turning point in world history.

And yet it is. Because this is what a durable administrative state looks like when it has settled into everyday life: not constant drama, but routine enforcement. A ruler can die. A dynasty can wobble. But a system that has taught people to live inside its measurements, its registers, and its expectations can persist and be inherited.

Beyond the city walls, caravans begin to gather for the west. Beyond the northern frontier, riders watch from open grasslands. Inside the palace, officials draft orders that will travel farther than a shout ever could.

24

The Eagle Ascendant

The wind off the northern river carries a smell the legionary has learned to distrust—wet earth, pine resin, smoke from fires he cannot see. He stands on a timber platform behind a palisade and watches the tree line. Beyond it lies a world Rome calls "barbarian," which mostly means a world that does not pay Roman taxes and does not accept Roman orders. His cloak is damp at the hem. His helmet pinches. The iron on his sword hilt is cold enough to sting.

Behind him the fort is a small city of discipline: barracks in straight lines, a granary raised off the ground, a headquarters building where orders are posted and punishments decided. In the distance a road runs like a promise through mud and forest, tying this edge back to the warm heart of the Mediterranean.

A generation ago, his grandfather might have fought for a republic that claimed to hate kings. Now he serves an emperor whose image is stamped on coins, whose name is spoken in prayers, whose authority reaches this frontier through paperwork and pay.

Rome did not become an empire because it wanted to betray its republican ideals. Rome became an empire because conquest solved problems in the short term and created deeper ones in the long term—until the republic's political machinery could not contain the wealth, violence, and ambition it had unleashed.

In its early centuries, Rome was one polis among many, a city-state in central Italy. It developed a republican system that balanced power among magistrates elected annually, a Senate dominated by elite families, and popular assemblies of citizens. It was never a democracy in the modern sense, and inequality was built into it. But it had a powerful internal myth: that no one man should be king, that Rome's liberty depended on shared rule and rotation of office. That myth mattered because it shaped how Romans talked about power even when power was shifting under their feet.

Rome's expansion began close to home, through alliances and wars that brought much of the Italian peninsula under Roman control by the early third century BCE. Then the horizon widened. The **Punic Wars** against Carthage (especially the Second, **218–201 BCE**) forced Rome into a wider Mediterranean struggle. By the second century BCE, Rome was defeating major Hellenistic powers, absorbing territories, and turning the Mediterranean into what later Romans would call *mare nostrum*—our sea.

Conquest brought spoils: gold, land, captives, and prestige. It also brought a problem that would corrode the republic from within: the republic's political system was designed for a city ruling nearby allies, not for a state controlling provinces across continents. The crisis did not arrive all at once. It accumulated like debt.

Roman commanders won wars and returned with armies loyal to them personally, not only to the state. Provincial governorships became opportunities for enrichment, because oversight was weak and the temptation was huge. Wealth flooded into elite hands, widening inequality.

Meanwhile, Rome's small farmers—the citizen backbone of the early republic—suffered. Long absences due to military service left farms neglected. Competition from large estates and cheap labor undercut smallholders. Many drifted into the city, where political leaders could feed and mobilize them. Cheap labor is an unblunt phrase for something sharper: slavery.

Rome's economy came to rely on enslaved people at an enormous scale, especially after major conquests produced floods of captives. Enslavement existed in earlier societies too, but Rome's combination of continuous conquest and an expanding market economy made slavery central, not peripheral. Enslaved people worked fields, mines, workshops, households, and construction sites. They were property under law, but they were also the human engine behind elite wealth and urban life.

You can see the empire in a single household when a freedperson steps into the street. He is legally free now, but freedom has layers. He has a Roman name—often his former owner's—because manumission ties him into a patron-client relationship that does not vanish at the moment of release. He can work, marry, earn, and in some contexts accumulate wealth. He can walk without fear of being sold. Yet he carries the mark of his origin in the social order, and his obligations to his patron remain real. If he succeeds, his children may rise further. If he fails, the old dependence can tighten again.

A freedperson's life captures one of Rome's most distinctive dynamics: a society that is brutally exploitative, yet unusually capable of absorbing outsiders into its legal and cultural framework over time. Rome is a machine of incorporation as well as domination. That machine will become one of its greatest strengths. But before that strength stabilizes, the republic convulses.

In the late second century BCE, reformers like the **Gracchi** attempted to address land inequality and the decline of smallholders. Their political battles ended in violence, signaling that the old norms of compromise were breaking. In the first century BCE, Rome endured a sequence of civil conflicts: the rivalry of **Marius and Sulla**, Sulla's dictatorship and proscriptions, and later the rise of powerful generals who could use military loyalty as political leverage.

The republic's institutions—elections, Senate debates, courts—kept functioning, but increasingly they functioned inside a climate of intimidation and faction. Politics became war by other means.

Then came the figure who turned the crisis into a point of no return: **Julius Caesar**.

Caesar's conquests in Gaul (mid-first century BCE) brought him immense wealth, loyal troops, and political fear among rivals. When tensions with the Senate escalated, he crossed the Rubicon in **49 BCE**, a symbolic act of civil war. After defeating rivals, he accumulated extraordinary power and was appointed dictator. His assassination in **44 BCE** was intended by conspirators as a restoration of liberty. Instead it opened a vacuum, and vacuums attract violence.

The struggle that followed—between Caesar's heirs and rivals—culminated in the rise of **Octavian**, later **Augustus**. After defeating Mark Antony and Cleopatra at **Actium (31 BCE)**, Octavian became the undisputed power. In **27 BCE**, he received titles and honors that signaled the new reality: Rome would continue to talk like a republic, but it would function like a monarchy.

Augustus was careful. He did not crown himself king. He claimed to restore the republic while quietly controlling the army, the provinces, and key offices. This was the Roman imperial trick: monarchy disguised in republican clothing, legitimacy built through tradition even as the structure changed.

From this settlement emerged the long period often called the **Pax Romana**, beginning in the late first century BCE and extending into the second century CE. "Peace" here does not mean the absence of violence. It means a reduction in internal civil war and a relative stability within the empire's core, enforced by Roman arms and administration.

For many, this stability was real. Roads were maintained. Trade moved across the Mediterranean with fewer interruptions. Cities expanded. Law became more standardized. Provincial elites could climb into Roman political life by adopting Roman norms and serving imperial administration. The empire became a framework in which local identities could persist while being woven into a wider order. But stability always has a cost, and the empire paid it at the edges.

Return to the legionary on the frontier. He is part of the cost. Forts like his line the Rhine, the Danube, the deserts of North Africa, the mountains of Britain and the Near East. The frontier is not a single wall; it is a zone of interaction: trade, diplomacy, raids, recruitment, intermarriage. Frontier societies form where Romans and non-Romans meet. A soldier might marry locally even if the law complicates it. Traders profit from supplying garrisons. Local leaders bargain for Roman favor. Enemies become auxiliaries. Auxiliaries become citizens over time.

This is where Rome's citizenship policy becomes one of its most powerful tools. Rome did not treat citizenship as a fixed ethnic identity. It treated it as a legal status that could be extended, granted, or earned. In the republic, Rome had already used graduated rights to bind Italian allies. After the **Social War (91–88 BCE)**—a conflict driven in part by Italian demands for citizenship—Rome extended citizenship broadly across Italy. In the imperial era, citizenship continued to spread, especially through military service and imperial grants. Citizenship was not pure generosity. It was strategy. Citizens had obligations—taxes, loyalty, service. They also had rights that made Roman rule more palatable to local elites. Incorporation reduced resistance and increased investment in the system.

You can watch this play out in a provincial city, inside a courtroom. A dispute is being heard—over property, inheritance, debt, a contract gone sour. The parties speak with accents. One wears a local style cloak; another has adopted Roman dress. A magistrate presides, perhaps a local official operating within Roman legal frameworks. The case is argued with documents and witnesses, and the language of law creates a shared arena where people from different backgrounds can compete without immediately reaching for violence.

Roman law was not always fair, and status mattered. But the existence of a legal system that could travel—courts, procedures, appeals—helped bind diverse provinces to the center. Law was a form of empire as much as legions were. Still, underneath the imperial peace lay pressures.

The slavery economy remained a moral and social fault line, producing wealth and cruelty, resistance and fear. Provincial extraction could be heavy, especially where governors were corrupt or where tax burdens were high. The army required constant funding, and emperors who lost military loyalty rarely kept their throne. Imperial succession was often unstable, even in "peaceful" times, because there was no purely constitutional method to choose the next ruler. The empire's stability depended on the continuous management of elites, armies, and provincial interests.

Rome's transformation, then, is not a clean story of progress from republic to empire. It is a story of scale. The republic's expansion created wealth, inequality, and militarized politics that its institutions could not absorb without changing. Civil war forced a new settlement. The empire stabilized the Mediterranean with roads, law, and a professional army, but it did so by concentrating power in one center and by relying on extraction and coercion that could turn brittle under stress. And yet, for centuries, it worked well enough to feel inevitable.

Return to the legionary again, watching the tree line. He is tired. He is paid. He is also far from home. Behind him, the empire hums—markets, courts, ports, temples, baths, amphitheaters—an enormous world stitched together by citizenship and force. In front of him, the forest holds its own politics, its own alliances and rivalries, its own reasons to trade or raid.

He tightens his cloak and listens for sounds that might mean trouble. Somewhere nearby, a trader's cart rattles toward the fort, carrying wine and tools and gossip. Somewhere in a city far to the south, a freedperson negotiates a contract, trying to turn legal status into a stable life. Somewhere in a provincial court, a judge pronounces a decision that will determine whose land stays whose.

Rome's empire is not only a conquest story. It is an everyday story of labor, law, and belonging—of who is inside, who is outside, and what it costs to cross that line.

25

Kingdoms of Sea and Sand

The man at the rope barrier does not look like a conqueror. He looks like someone who has spent a lifetime watching other people move. His shade is a strip of cloth stretched between two poles at the edge of the track, where the hard ground begins to soften into sand. A line of pack animals waits with heads low, blinking against grit. Leather creaks. Water sloshes in skins. A driver shifts his weight and glances toward the horizon, measuring time the way desert people do, in heat and distance rather than hours.

On a low table sits a simple kit: a set of weights, a small seal, a board marked with notches. The toll is not outrageous, but it is unavoidable. Pay, and the caravan passes to the next well. Refuse, and you have a problem that grows larger with every mile of thirst ahead. Coins change hands. A receipt is scratched out or a token pressed into clay. The barrier lifts. The animals start forward, and the toll-keeper watches them go as if he is watching a river flow.

This is one way Africa enters classical history: not as a backdrop, not as an empty space between "civilized" worlds, but as a manager of movement. A gatekeeper on a route. A broker at a port. A ruler whose inscription makes a claim in stone. In the classical age, Africa is central because Africa sits on the hinge points of trade and empire—Mediterranean shores that fed Rome and resisted it, river corridors that carried gold and grain, and a Red Sea that served as an artery between the Roman world, Arabia, and India.

If you want to understand how the classical world worked, you have to stop imagining Africa as an edge. It was a center of gravity.

Start on the Mediterranean coast, where the sea looks calm until you remember how quickly ships can turn it into a battlefield.

Long before Rome was an empire, **Carthage** was a commercial powerhouse. Founded as a Phoenician colony (traditionally dated to the late ninth century BCE), it grew into a maritime state whose strength came from ships, harbors, and a web of trading posts. Carthage's reach stretched along North Africa's coastline, toward Iberia, and through island stepping stones like Sicily and Sardinia. It did not need to conquer like an inland empire to become rich. It needed to control chokepoints, manage alliances, and keep the sea lanes working.

That sea-lane world produced a particular kind of power. Carthage could project force quickly where ships could go, and it could pay for war through trade. It also relied on the resources of the African hinterland—grain, livestock, labor—and on relationships with local communities who were never simply "subjects" in a neat imperial sense. North Africa was already politically crowded: towns, tribal confederations, shifting coalitions, and rulers who understood the land better than any sailor did. Carthage was strong, but it was not alone. Rome's rise turned that Mediterranean balance into a duel.

The **Punic Wars** were not only wars between two states; they were wars over the structure of the Mediterranean itself—who would control key islands, who would tax commerce, who would decide which ships sailed safely and which did not. The **Second Punic War (218–201 BCE)** still casts a long shadow because of Hannibal's march into Italy, a campaign so audacious it feels like a myth even when you know it happened. But the deeper transformation came from the outcome. Rome did not simply defeat Carthage. Rome learned to fight at sea, to sustain long wars, and to treat overseas territory as something that could be held and administered.

Carthage's final destruction in **146 BCE** is often narrated as a clean end. In reality, it was the end of one political era and the beginning of another. Rome gained an African foothold that would become one of its most productive provincial zones. The land that had fed Carthage would help feed Rome. That is the bitter continuity of empire: the fields stay, the rulers change, and the surplus keeps moving north.

Between Carthage and Rome stood a power that mattered precisely because it was not a simple pawn: **Numidia**.

Numidia was not one uniform "tribe." It was a region of Berber-speaking communities and political formations that could unite under strong leaders and fragment again under pressure. During Rome's struggle with Carthage, Numidian cavalry became famous—fast, effective, difficult for heavy infantry to control. Leaders like **Masinissa** (reigned roughly **c. 202–148 BCE**) used the moment brilliantly. Masinissa allied with Rome against Carthage, expanded Numidian power, and built a kingdom that benefitted from both Mediterranean connections and inland control.

This is the pattern you see again and again in African history: local powers using imperial rivalries as leverage, not simply being crushed by them. Masinissa gained territory and legitimacy through alliance, but he was also building a state with its own ambitions, its own agriculture, its own taxes, its own elite networks.

Rome, for its part, learned another imperial lesson in Numidia: conquest is not always the fastest way to win. Sometimes corruption does the work for you.

The **Jugurthine War (112–105 BCE)**, sparked by the Numidian king **Jugurtha** and Rome's entanglement in local succession disputes, exposed how vulnerable the Roman Republic had become to bribery and faction. Roman commanders were accused of taking payments, delaying action, and turning war into a revenue stream. The scandal helped fuel political tensions back in Rome, the kind of tensions that would later explode into civil war. Here, Africa is not peripheral. Africa is a stage on which Roman politics rots in public view.

By the time Rome's imperial structure stabilized, North Africa had become one of its key engines: grain production, urban growth, and wealth that circulated through imperial markets. Yet even then, the region was not simply "Roman." Frontier zones remained zones: of trade, conflict, accommodation, and identity mixing. African elites could become Roman citizens and Roman patrons; Roman soldiers could settle and marry locally; and the countryside could still feel the weight of extraction. Empire was never just a flag. It was a daily negotiation over land, labor, and law.

Now turn away from the Mediterranean's blue and look south and east, where Africa's other great classical sphere ran on heat, wind, and water. The Nile corridor connected Egypt to inner Africa, and the Red Sea connected that corridor to Arabia and the Indian Ocean. In that network stood the kingdom of **Kush**, and later its southern center at **Meroë**.

Kush had a long history, including periods when Nubian kings ruled Egypt itself in the eighth and seventh centuries BCE. But by the time Rome was rising, Kush's political center had shifted south from Napata to Meroë (a process often placed around the early first millennium BCE). Meroë sat in a landscape that could tap multiple routes: the Nile, caravan paths, and connections toward the Red Sea. It was well positioned to act as a broker of African wealth—especially **gold and ivory**, along with exotic animals, incense, and other high-value goods moving between ecological zones.

Meroë's material culture tells you it was no mere tributary. It had its own monumental architecture, its own distinctive pyramid fields, and its own writing system—the **Meroitic script**—which remains only partially understood. That partial silence matters. It reminds you that much of Africa's classical history is filtered through outsiders' texts: Greek, Roman, Egyptian. Where the local record is hard to read, the temptation is to treat the society as less complex. That is a historian's mistake. Meroë built, ruled, traded, and fought. It did not need Rome's approval to be real. And Meroë did fight.

When Rome took Egypt in **30 BCE**, it inherited a frontier at the Nile's southern edge.

Frontier politics quickly turned sharp. In the late first century BCE, conflict flared between Roman Egypt and Kush, associated in many accounts with a Kushite queen titled **Kandake** (Candace in older sources). Roman forces and Kushite forces clashed, forts were attacked, and the frontier became a testing ground for two states with very different geographies but equal understanding of leverage. The end result, after fighting and negotiation (often dated around **24–22 BCE** for the main conflict phase), was a settlement that appears to have stabilized relations for a time. Rome did not simply swallow Kush. Kush remained a power on the southern corridor, able to bargain, resist, and trade.

Trade is where the Red Sea becomes unavoidable. By the early Roman imperial era, merchants from Roman Egypt were sailing down the Red Sea in increasing numbers, using knowledge of the **monsoon winds** to cross the Indian Ocean more predictably. The Roman state benefitted from this commerce through customs and taxes. Egyptian ports on the Red Sea, connected to the Nile by desert roads, became crucial nodes—places where goods were shifted from ship to camel to riverboat and onward.

This is where a port ledger tells you more than a battle ever could. Picture a customs office in a Red Sea port, perhaps in the Roman era at a place like **Berenike** or **Myos Hormos**, where desert heat presses down and everything smells faintly of salt and animal sweat. Under an awning, a clerk works with ink and papyrus, or with whatever record system the office uses, marking shipments as they arrive: amphorae of wine, sacks of grain, bundles of textiles, jars of oil. And then the exotic items that make the whole route worth the risk: ivory tusks, tortoise shell, aromatic resins, gemstones, pepper and spices coming from farther east.

The clerk's job is not romantic. He is there to make movement legible to the state. He records quantities. He assesses duties. He stamps approvals. He turns wind and courage and ocean skill into revenue.

Those ledgers—whether preserved directly or reconstructed through texts and archaeology—reveal a classical truth: Africa was not merely supplying Rome with raw material. Africa was a vital corridor that made Rome part of a wider Afro-Eurasian economy. The Red Sea trade tied the Mediterranean to Arabia and India, and African goods were among the most valued cargo. **Ivory** was not a side note; it was a major luxury commodity. **Gold** was not only ornament; it was money, diplomacy, and state power condensed into metal.

Then, further south along the Red Sea and into the Horn of Africa, another kingdom rose that understood this geography with exceptional clarity: **Aksum**.

From roughly the first centuries CE onward, **Aksum** (in the region of modern Eritrea and northern Ethiopia) grew into a state whose power rested on highland agriculture, control of routes, and participation in Red Sea and Indian Ocean commerce. Aksum's port, often identified with **Adulis**, was a critical gateway. Goods moved down from the interior to the coast: gold, ivory, animal products, and more. Goods moved in from across the sea: fine textiles, metals, wine, luxury items, and the kinds of prestige commodities that make elite politics run smoothly.

Aksum's rulers did what durable states often do when they reach confidence: they minted coins and carved claims into stone. Coinage matters because it signals more than wealth. It signals administrative reach and the ability to standardize exchange. Coins travel. They carry a ruler's image and titles into markets where his soldiers may never stand. They say: this is whose authority underwrites value.

And then there is the royal inscription, the moment power speaks directly. Aksumite inscriptions—some in Greek, some in local scripts—present kings not as minor chiefs but as rulers of a wide realm, making claims about conquest, order, and divine favor. One of the most famous Aksumite rulers, **Ezana** (commonly dated to the fourth century CE), is associated with inscriptions that reflect military campaigns and, crucially, a shift in religious identity as Aksum adopted **Christianity**. Here again Africa is not "late" to history; it is a place where global religious transformations take institutional form early, tied to state power and cross-sea connections.

Aksum's position also made it a player in Arabian politics. In later centuries, Aksumite rulers intervened across the Red Sea in South Arabia, showing that the Red Sea was not a boundary but a bridge. The same waters that carried merchants also carried armies and diplomats. Step back now and the pattern across Africa's classical spheres becomes clear.

In the Mediterranean zone, Carthage and Rome competed for dominance, but their contest was shaped by African realities—by local alliances, by cavalry, by inland routes, by the agricultural wealth of North Africa. Numidia was not a footnote; it was a decisive actor, and the wars around it fed back into Roman political crises.

In the Nile and Red Sea zone, Kush and later Aksum anchored trade routes that made African goods central to Mediterranean and Indian Ocean worlds. Roman Egypt did not simply extract from the south. It negotiated, fought, and traded across a frontier with real power on the other side. The Red Sea trade did not simply "bring the East to Rome." It ran through African and Arabian nodes that profited, regulated, and shaped what could move.

And at every point, **gold and ivory** tell the story's backbone. They are the commodities that move because they compress value. They are the goods that justify dangerous routes. They are the prizes that states want to tax, control, and display.

Return to the toll-keeper at the rope barrier. He knows nothing of Roman Senate debates. He may never hear the name of a Kushite queen or an Aksumite king. But his work is part of the same system. By taking a fee, he funds protection or a local ruler's authority. By controlling passage, he shapes which goods reach the coast, which ports flourish, which merchants gain advantage. He turns geography into power the way empires do, but at a smaller scale.

Far away, in a Red Sea port, a clerk closes a ledger and seals it. A shipment has been recorded. Taxes have been assessed. The state has taken its share of the wind. And in the highlands, a royal inscription catches the sun and announces a ruler's name to the future, insisting that this kingdom belongs in the world's memory.

Africa in the classical age was not a silent continent waiting to be "connected." It was already connecting others—through coasts and corridors, through markets and frontiers, through the hard, human work of controlling movement.

26

Early American States

The rubber ball hits the stone court with a sound that carries—hollow, sharp, oddly alive. Men move in quick bursts under the heavy sun, hips turning, shoulders braced, hands held back because the rules demand a certain kind of control. The court is long and narrow, its walls rising on either side like a channel meant to focus not water, but attention. Faces in the crowd tilt forward. Some have come for sport, some for ritual, some because this is where power shows itself without needing to speak. The ball skids, rebounds, threatens to roll dead, then springs up again as a player throws his body into the moment, driving it forward with a practiced strike.

From far away, it might look like a game. From inside the society that built the court, it is also a display of order—discipline imposed on chance, a contest staged in stone, a public event where winners and losers can carry meanings that outlast the sweat.

In Eurasia, early states often rose around river valleys thick with grain and draft animals, and they advertised power through palaces, chariots, and writing that recorded taxes and laws. In the Americas, complex societies rose along different paths. They built cities without horses. They engineered landscapes without iron plows. They produced monumental art, dense ritual calendars, and powerful states on the back of maize, beans, squash, and potatoes; on irrigation canals and terraced hillsides; on human labor organized at scale; and on legitimacy expressed through ceremony as much as through bureaucratic documents. None of this was "late" history. It was history on its own terms.

By **1500 BCE**, along the Gulf Coast lowlands of what is now Mexico, communities were already creating something that later Mesoamerican societies would recognize as foundational. Archaeologists call this world **Olmec**, not because we know what its people called themselves, but because later names had to fill a gap. Sites such as **San Lorenzo** (flourishing roughly **c. 1400–1000 BCE**) and **La Venta** (prominent roughly **c. 900–400 BCE**) show organized labor and elite power made visible: massive earthworks, carefully planned ceremonial centers, long-distance exchange in prestige goods like jade, and the famous colossal stone heads—faces carved at a scale that makes you understand, instantly, that someone could command quarrying, transport, and skilled work far beyond household needs.

The Olmec legacy is not a single invention you can point to and label as "the beginning." It is a style of doing power: sacred centers laid out with intention; imagery of rulers, animals, and cosmology; and networks that carried objects and ideas across regions. Later Mesoamerican cultures would build their own systems, often very different in detail, but they lived in a landscape where earlier forms of ritual authority had already proven they could gather people and hold them in a shared world of symbols.

Move inland to the Valley of Oaxaca, and you can see an early state making a different, bolder choice about geography.

Around **500 BCE**, a major center was founded on a mountain ridge: **Monte Albán**, the capital of a society we call **Zapotec**. Building a city on a hilltop is a statement. It is less convenient for water and farming than valley floors. It is harder to haul materials up. People do not do it by accident. They do it when visibility, defense, and dominance matter enough to justify the cost.

From Monte Albán's heights, you can look across the valley like a ruler looks across subjects. The city's plazas and monumental buildings reorganized the landscape into a political theater. Early carved stones known as the "Danzantes" show human figures in poses that have long been debated; many scholars interpret them as defeated captives or enemies, displayed as warnings and trophies rather than dancers in celebration. Whether every figure represents a conquest is uncertain, but the message of the art is not gentle. Monte Albán is announcing that force and hierarchy now have a home.

This is also where writing begins to step into clearer view. Zapotec inscriptions are among the earliest writing systems in the Americas, appearing by the late first millennium BCE. They are not long histories like later Maya texts, but they suggest a political world that wants names, dates, and events fixed beyond memory. In a society where alliances shift and conquest matters, writing becomes one more way to make power durable.

To the east and north, in the lowlands of the Yucatán and Guatemala, another civilization was growing in a landscape that did not reward easy urban life.

The **Maya** world is often associated with its Classic-era cities and stelae after **250 CE**, but the foundations were laid earlier, in the **Preclassic** period. By the late first millennium BCE and early centuries CE, large centers such as **El Mirador** in the Petén region were building monumental complexes—vast platforms and pyramids—on a scale that still surprises people who assume early American cities were small until "later."

What makes Maya urbanism especially striking is the environment. Much of the lowland Maya region has seasonal water challenges. Rain falls heavily in certain months and disappears in others. Rivers are not always conveniently navigable where the largest cities grew. So Maya complexity depended not only on temples and rulers, but on managing water and land in sophisticated ways: reservoirs, cisterns, modified wetlands, and the careful use of bajos and uplands. In some regions, communities built and maintained systems that could store rainwater for dry seasons and support dense populations.

That kind of landscape engineering is easy to miss if you only look for canals like Mesopotamia's or river corridors like Egypt's. But the logic is the same: if you can control water, you can stabilize food. If you can stabilize food, you can support specialists—builders, artisans, priests, administrators. If you can support specialists, you can build institutions that outlast a single harvest.

In Mesoamerica, state power often expressed itself through ritual and public spectacle—ballgames, calendrical ceremonies, processions, offerings. That does not mean these states lacked coercion. They fought wars, took captives, and enforced hierarchy. It means legitimacy traveled through sacred time as much as through written law. Rulers did not only command; they performed a role that linked the community to the cosmos, to ancestors, to the terrifying uncertainty of rain, disease, and fertility.

Now shift thousands of kilometers south, to the Pacific coast of Peru, where desert meets ocean and rivers cut narrow green valleys through otherwise harsh land.

Here, in the Andes, complex societies rose with their own distinctive tools and constraints. The coast could be extraordinarily productive because of marine resources, but farming depended on controlling river water that arrived seasonally and could be redirected through canals. Inland, different elevations offered different crops and pastures. The Andean world became an engineering world, not because Andeans loved engineering as an abstract idea, but because ecology demanded it.

By the early centuries CE, the **Moche** civilization flourished along several northern Peruvian valleys (commonly dated roughly **c. 100–800 CE**). Moche power was not centralized in a single capital the way people sometimes imagine; it likely consisted of multiple valley polities with shared cultural forms and competing elites. Yet the shared forms were strong: monumental adobe platforms like the **Huaca del Sol** and **Huaca de la Luna** near the Moche Valley; fine ceramics that depict scenes of ritual, warfare, and daily life with unsettling clarity; and irrigation works that turned desert edges into fields.

Moche art is one of the most vivid windows into early American ritual and violence. Painted and modeled scenes show prisoners stripped and led in lines, ceremonies involving blood, elites in elaborate regalia. It would be a mistake to treat every depiction as a literal documentary photograph. Art has its own language. But the repetition is telling. Moche power seems tightly bound to warfare and ritual display, with elite authority reinforced through control over water, labor, and sacred performance.

You can feel the weight of that authority in a burial.

In the late twentieth century, archaeologists uncovered the richly furnished tombs at **Sipán** in Peru's Lambayeque region, dating to the Moche era. The details of the grave goods—ornaments, masks, weapons, attendants—show an elite world built on rank so steep that even death becomes a stage for power. A ruler is not buried alone. He is buried with the social structure around him, arranged as if hierarchy itself must continue in the ground.

If the Moche show one route to Andean state formation—irrigation, ritual authority, militarized elites—then the **Nazca** show another kind of power written directly onto the landscape.

In the arid plains of southern Peru, the **Nazca** culture (often dated roughly **c. 100 BCE–800 CE**) is famous for the geoglyphs: long straight lines, trapezoids, and figures of animals and plants etched into the desert surface by removing darker stones to reveal lighter ground beneath. Seen from above, the designs are astonishing. Seen from the ground, they can feel abstract—lines stretching toward the horizon with a calm insistence.

One of the most disciplined ways to approach the Nazca lines is to resist the urge to solve them with a single dramatic answer. They likely served multiple roles over time: ritual pathways, offerings to deities associated with water and fertility, sacred geography that linked communities to place and sky. In a landscape where water is precious and unpredictable, marking the desert in ways that align movement, ceremony, and cosmology makes a harsh kind of sense. And Nazca ingenuity was not only symbolic. It was practical.

In parts of the Nazca region, people built underground aqueduct systems often called **puquios**—spiraling access points leading to channels that helped bring water to fields. The precise dating and spread of these systems is still studied, and not every feature belongs neatly to the same moment, but the broader fact remains: Nazca communities invested in water management that allowed agriculture to persist in difficult conditions. Their lines and their channels belong to the same logic: survival secured by collective work, made meaningful through ritual.

Across both Mesoamerica and the Andes, land and water management was not a footnote. It was politics.

A canal is an argument about who gets water first. A terrace is a claim about who controls labor. A reservoir is a decision about which neighborhoods will drink in the dry season. A raised field or managed wetland is proof that planning can be embedded in soil. These systems required coordination, maintenance, and authority—sometimes cooperative, sometimes coercive, often both. They also created vulnerabilities. When climate patterns shifted, when droughts hit, when floods came too hard, the systems could strain. And when systems strain, legitimacy is tested. If rulers claim sacred power over rain and fertility, they are judged by the sky.

So how do these early American states fit into a world history that is often written with Eurasian assumptions?

First, they remind us that cities and states do not require the same technological package everywhere. The Americas developed urban and state complexity without horses, without wheeled transport used at scale for hauling, and without Old World-style plow agriculture. They did it through dense farming systems, human labor organized across communities, and political-religious institutions capable of sustaining long-term projects. They also developed forms of writing and calendrical science in Mesoamerica that would become among the most sophisticated in the ancient world, even if in this chapter we are still in the earlier phases of those developments.

Second, they show that ritual is not the opposite of administration. In many early American contexts, ritual was administration's ally. A public ceremony can mobilize labor and align people's expectations. A sacred calendar can schedule social life. A ballgame can dramatize hierarchy and cosmic order. When you lack certain bureaucratic tools, you often strengthen the tools you do have: performance, spectacle, memory, architecture, the disciplined repetition of communal acts.

Third, they emphasize that state power was not uniform. There was no single "American empire" in this era. There were many polities with different structures—some strongly centralized, some networked, some city-based, some valley-based—connected through trade and shared religious ideas. Goods traveled: obsidian, jade, shells, feathers, textiles, metals in later Andean phases, cacao and other prestige items in

Mesoamerica. With goods traveled styles, symbols, and political techniques.

Return to the ballcourt. The match ends, and the crowd's energy shifts into story. The players step away with bruises blooming under protection gear. In the court's stone, the day's contest becomes part of a longer rhythm: seasonal cycles, ritual calendars, alliances affirmed, tensions displayed without immediate war—or, sometimes, with war's shadow close enough that everyone understands the stakes.

Far to the south, the Nazca desert holds its lines under a sun that rarely forgives. A figure carved into the earth waits for feet to trace it again in ceremony, or for rain to justify the prayers that shaped the path. In a Moche valley, a canal carries water past fields that only exist because someone organized the digging, the repairs, the rules. In a tomb, a ruler lies wrapped in wealth that is also a political document, declaring hierarchy to the living through the arrangement of the dead.

These are early states, but not early in any childish sense. They are mature answers to mature problems: how to feed many people, how to make strangers cooperate, how to turn landscape into security, how to persuade and compel at the same time.

27

Roads, Ships, and Camels

The sailor watches the sky the way a farmer watches soil—reading it for promise and danger. The sea off the coast is calm, almost too calm, a pane of gray-blue that seems to hold its breath. In the harbor, the ship's rigging taps softly, a restless sound like teeth chattering. The crew has been waiting for weeks, not because the cargo is missing, but because the wind is wrong. Everything depends on timing. Leave too early and you fight the ocean until your water runs out. Leave too late and you arrive after the market has shifted, after the season's profit has been claimed by someone bolder or luckier.

Then, one morning, the air changes. It is subtle—more pressure in the breeze, a different taste of moisture, a shift in how the clouds stack on the horizon. The sailor's face lifts. He does not need a priest to tell him this is the moment. The monsoon has turned.

He calls down to the dock. Ropes tighten. Sails are checked. The ship pushes out, not into emptiness, but into a system as reliable as any road—if you know how to read it.

By the time we reach the early centuries of the first millennium BCE and then into the first centuries CE, the world's great empires and city networks are no longer isolated puzzles. They are parts of "small worlds": regions where people, goods, and ideas move often enough that distant places start to feel connected, not mythical. The connections are not global in the modern sense. They are uneven, seasonal, and dangerous. But they are strong enough to do something transformative: they spread wealth and techniques, religions and fashions—and sometimes disease—along the same routes that carry grain and silk.

Movement is not a backdrop to history. It is one of history's engines. Roads and ships, camels and caravanserais, brokers and interpreters—these are the tools that make large-scale society possible and make it vulnerable.

Start with the Roman world, where movement was carved into stone and stamped into routine.

A Roman road is not just a path. It is a statement. It runs straight when it can, and when it cannot, it cuts through hills with labor that makes geography submit. It is layered—stone, gravel, packed earth—built to last, built to carry weight. Along it are milestones and waystations, bridges and culverts, a whole vocabulary of infrastructure that says: Rome intends to be present tomorrow.

Roads served the army first. Legions needed to move quickly, supplies needed to follow, messengers needed to carry orders across provinces. But once a road exists, everyone uses it: tax collectors, merchants, pilgrims, runaways, entertainers, officials seeking promotion, families migrating to a new town. A road compresses distance. It also compresses differences. It forces encounters—between languages, laws, and customs—that would otherwise remain separate. And Rome's roads did not end at land's edge.

Sea lanes were just as important. The Mediterranean was a highway of grain ships and merchant convoys, coastal craft and long-haul vessels. Rome depended on maritime supply for survival, especially the grain that fed cities like Rome itself. Ports became nodes of empire, places where customs were collected and disputes mediated, where sailors carried gossip faster than official dispatches.

The Roman state did not control every wave, but it did shape maritime movement through naval power, anti-piracy efforts in certain periods, and the infrastructure of ports and warehouses. And Rome's legal and monetary systems made trade less risky for those inside the empire's umbrella. A merchant could rely, often, on standardized coinage, predictable courts, and a web of cities where "Roman" norms—weights, measures, contracts—were familiar enough to be usable.

That predictability created prosperity. It also created interdependence. When grain routes failed, cities starved. When pirates surged, prices jumped. When disease entered a port, it could move inland on the same roads that carried tax revenue.

Now widen the lens south and east, to the Indian Ocean, where the road is not paved stone but wind.

The monsoon system—seasonal winds that reverse direction—made regular long-distance sailing across the Indian Ocean possible for those who learned its rhythm. This was not guesswork. It was accumulated knowledge: when the winds shift, how currents behave, where storms cluster, which months favor crossings. Sailors who understood this could travel between the Red Sea and Indian ports, between Arabian coasts and East Africa, between India and Southeast Asia, in relatively predictable seasonal cycles.

This changed the logic of trade. Instead of hugging coasts endlessly, ships could cross open water with purpose. Ports became seasonal theaters: crowded during the right wind, quiet during the wrong one. Merchants began to time their lives to the atmosphere. Whole communities became experts in waiting, then moving fast.

A sailor's monsoon timing was not just practical; it was economic power. Arrive early with the right cargo—pepper, textiles, aromatics, ivory, gemstones—and you could set prices. Arrive late and you took what was left. In this way, wind shaped wealth, and wealth shaped politics. States along these routes could tax trade, protect harbors, and build legitimacy through prosperity. And religious ideas could travel with merchants, because a ship's hold has room not only for goods but for people, songs, stories, and practices.

But oceans, for all their drama, are not the only highways. Between empires and seas lay deserts and steppe corridors where movement demanded a different technology: the camel.

The domesticated camel—especially the dromedary in Arabia and the Bactrian camel in Central Asia—transformed desert logistics. A camel can go longer without water than a horse, carry heavy loads, and survive in environments that punish other animals. With camels, deserts stopped being absolute barriers and became difficult corridors. Difficult is not the same as impossible. And once movement is possible, someone will monetize it.

This is where oasis brokers enter the story. An oasis is not simply water. It is a market, a refuge, a checkpoint. It is where caravans rest, repair, and exchange information. It is also where local powers—tribal confederations, city authorities, imperial outposts—can extract tolls and offer protection. In the spaces between empires, oasis brokers become indispensable intermediaries. They know routes. They know languages. They know which bandit groups are active this season and which have been paid off. They know how to negotiate safe passage and how to read the shifting politics of the desert.

To outsiders, such brokers can look like minor figures on the margins. In reality, they can be kingmakers, because empires need corridors more than corridors need empires. If your silk, your spices, your horses, your slaves, your precious metals must pass through a chokepoint, the person who controls that chokepoint has leverage.

In Central Asia and the Middle East, caravan routes linked the Mediterranean world to Iran, to steppe confederations, to India, and to the edges of Han China's western corridors. No single empire controlled the entire chain for long. The chain was held together by negotiation: taxes, bribes, treaties, marriages, hostage exchanges, and the shared understanding that trade can enrich even enemies.

And the nightly life of that chain is best seen in a caravanserai. Night drops quickly in the desert. Heat drains away. The sky becomes sharp with stars, as if someone has scrubbed it clean. A caravanserai—an inn-fortress for traders—glows with firelight behind its walls. Inside, animals are watered and fed. Men loosen their belts and sit with bowls of stew. Someone recites a prayer in one language; someone answers in another. The air smells of sweat, smoke, and dung, but also of spices when a merchant opens a bundle to check that moisture hasn't spoiled it.

This is where routes become social worlds. Information travels here: which king has died, which border is closed, which port is dangerous, which coin is being debased, which plague rumor is true. Trust is negotiated over meals. Disputes are settled or postponed. Partnerships are formed between strangers who will rely on each other across hundreds of kilometers.

And in those partnerships, diasporas become powerful. Merchants often traveled in communities—families or religious groups spread across multiple cities—because trust is a precious currency when you cannot sue a stranger in a distant land. Diaspora networks created reliable nodes: a cousin in a port who could store goods, a co-religionist who could vouch for a contract, a community elder who could arbitrate a dispute without involving hostile authorities. Jewish communities in the Mediterranean, merchant groups across the Indian Ocean, and many other trading diasporas served as connective tissue in these small worlds. They were not outside the system. They were part of what made the system work.

In the middle of all these networks stands the multilingual trader, the person who makes connection real. He is in a port city where the crowd is a moving mosaic. He hears Latin on one side, Greek on the other, Egyptian or Aramaic in the middle, and perhaps a sailor's rough Arabic, and he answers in whichever tongue will make the deal smoother. He knows how to calculate exchange rates. He knows which weights are honest and which are shaved. He knows which official can be bribed and which must be respected. He knows that an insult can cost more than a tariff.

He is not a ruler, but he moves through rulers' worlds. He is one of the people who turn empires into economies and economies into culture.

The effects of these movement systems were enormous, and not always benign.

Goods moved, and with goods came technologies: ship designs, navigational practices, metallurgical techniques, glassmaking, textile patterns. Ideas moved: religious teachings, philosophical concepts, artistic styles. Stories moved: myths, epics, rumors, political propaganda. People moved: soldiers, slaves, migrants, pilgrims, scholars. Some movement was chosen. Much of it was forced.

And pathogens moved too. When roads and sea lanes become reliable, so do disease routes. A virus or bacterium does not care about citizenship or scripture. It cares about bodies in contact. A crowded port, a marching army, a caravanserai where dozens sleep close under one roof—these are perfect environments for transmission. The same connectivity that makes wealth and learning possible also makes epidemics more plausible and more wide-reaching.

This is why "small worlds" matter. A small world is not a peaceful village. It is a region where distance has been reduced enough that events in one place can ripple into another: a grain shortage becoming political unrest; a war disrupting trade and raising prices; a new faith gaining followers through merchant contacts; a disease spreading along a route that never sleeps.

So what changed, fundamentally, in this era of roads, ships, and camels?

First, movement became more routine. Not safe, not universal, not modern—but frequent enough to build expectations.

Second, intermediaries gained power. The sailor who reads the monsoon, the oasis broker who controls a well, the diaspora elder who guarantees a contract, the market inspector who standardizes measures—these people shape history as much as kings do, because they shape what can flow and what gets stuck.

Third, cultural worlds began to overlap. A person could live in a city where multiple gods were worshiped, multiple languages spoken, multiple legal traditions negotiated. Identity could become layered: local by birth, imperial by citizenship, religious by choice, commercial by necessity.

Return to the sailor. His ship is now far from land, riding a wind that feels almost alive in the canvas. The ocean's surface changes color through the day, from steel to sapphire to black. He cannot control the monsoon. He can only understand it and gamble his life on its patterns. In a way, that is what every empire and every trader is doing too—trying to read the forces larger than themselves, then building systems that make those forces usable.

On land, in a caravanserai, a fire burns low and a camel coughs in its sleep. Somewhere a multilingual trader counts coins by touch in the dark, listening to a stranger's story and deciding whether to believe it. These routes are not just lines on a map. They are the veins and nerves of the classical world.

Part V

Late Antiquity & World Religions (c. 200–600 CE)

28

Twilight of Rome

Smoke clung to the alleyways near the mint, turning afternoon light into something bruised and yellow. In the streets of Rome, men ran with the desperate rhythm of people who know the state has turned against them. You could hear it before you saw it: a harsh roar rolling between stone walls, the crack of shields, the dull punch of bodies hitting pavement. Somewhere a fire took in a stack of wooden frames; sparks lifted and vanished into the haze. A crowd surged, then broke, then surged again—workers, soldiers, bystanders—each wave pulling more people into its panic.

This was not a foreign invasion. This was not a civil war between rival emperors at the edge of the map. This was the empire's own machinery stuttering inside its capital.

In the early **270s CE**, Rome was trying to repair a broken currency and a broken trust. Emperor **Aurelian**—a soldier-emperor who fought to stitch the empire back together—pushed monetary reforms. Ancient sources, uneven in reliability, suggest the reforms helped spark a violent revolt connected to the mint. Whether every detail is true or not, the shape of the moment fits what we know: by the third century, money had become an anxious, political substance. When coinage was debased, prices jumped, soldiers grumbled, and cities trembled. When reforms came, they could feel like punishment to those who had profited from the old rot.

Rome's transformation begins here, not in a church or a palace, but in the pressure points where the state touches ordinary life: pay, bread, order in the streets.

The **third-century crisis**—usually dated from **235 to 284 CE**—was not one disaster but a sustained stress test. In **235**, Emperor **Alexander Severus** was killed by his troops, and what followed was a churn of rulers elevated by armies and cut down by rivals. Frontiers buckled under pressure from multiple directions. In the east, the **Sasanian** dynasty replaced the Parthians and fought Rome with renewed force; in **260**, Emperor **Valerian** was captured by the Persians, an event so shocking it felt like a cosmic humiliation. In the west and in the eastern provinces, the empire fractured into breakaway regimes—the **Gallic Empire** (beginning around **260**) and the **Palmyrene** sphere under leaders associated with **Zenobia**—not because everyone suddenly stopped being Roman, but because the central government could not reliably protect and pay.

Disease and economy added their own weight. A devastating epidemic often called the **Plague of Cyprian** spread in the mid-third century, deepening fear and weakening manpower. Coinage debasement accelerated as emperors minted more money to pay troops without the metal to back it. Inflation, shortages, and tax strain were felt most sharply in cities, where survival depended on steady supply lines.

The old imperial story—Rome bringing order outward—began to reverse. Now order had to be forced inward, rebuilt, defended against collapse from within.

Aurelian's reign (**270–275**) was one of the first attempts to impose that rebuilding through sheer energy. He defeated breakaway powers and reasserted control across large portions of the empire. He also began fortifying the capital with what we now call the **Aurelian Walls**, a sign that even Rome itself was no longer assumed safe. When an empire starts walling its heart, it is admitting something: the world it commands has become less predictable than the world it fears. But soldier-emperors could not solve a structural problem with battlefield victories alone. The crisis demanded something more permanent: a re-engineering of how the empire governed, taxed, and defended.

That re-engineering came under **Diocletian**, who took power in **284**.

Diocletian did not pretend the old style of rule could simply be restored. He treated the empire like a body too large for one pair of hands. His answer was the **Tetrarchy**—rule divided among two senior emperors (Augusti) and two junior emperors (Caesares). It was not democracy. It was an attempt to keep succession orderly and response time fast. Emperors could be nearer to frontiers, closer to the crises that bred mutiny and secession.

He also reorganized administration: more provinces, layered oversight, tighter control. The empire became more bureaucratic because the empire had to become more bureaucratic. It needed clearer tax extraction, more predictable provisioning, better records, a state capable of seeing its population as units of labor and revenue.

Taxes shifted toward payment **in kind**—grain, animals, cloth—because coin could not be trusted the way it once was. Price edicts, including the famous but difficult-to-enforce **Edict on Maximum Prices (301)**, reflected a government trying to pin down an economy that no longer behaved. The state's presence thickened in daily life: registers, requisitions, officials who measured and demanded.

And the army changed shape with the new state. Soldiers had always been central to Roman power, but now they became central to Roman survival. More troops were stationed along frontiers. Mobile field forces became more important. Forts and supply depots multiplied. The empire learned to defend not only with walls and legions, but with logistics—roads repaired for troop movement, grain redirected to feed garrisons, the entire fiscal system bent toward the needs of war.

You can feel the transformation in a soldier's pay. At a frontier post, a man waits in line while an officer reads names from a list. He receives a portion in coin—worth less, sometimes, than it was in his father's day—and a portion in goods: grain, oil, perhaps a cloth allotment. The state is feeding him because it cannot always trust money to do the feeding. He knows what he is owed, and he knows what the state can actually deliver are not always the same. Around him, men talk in low voices about the price of bread in the nearest town, about rumors of enemy movement, about whether the next emperor will keep promises or die before the season changes. Pay is not just compensation. It is loyalty made tangible. When it fails, armies make emperors and unmake them.

Diocletian's reforms bought time and stability, but they did not settle the deeper question of legitimacy. An empire can be reorganized. It still needs a story strong enough to hold it together. That is where sacred politics begins to rise from the background to the center.

In earlier Roman centuries, religion had been plural and pragmatic. The empire absorbed gods the way it absorbed provinces, offering room for many cults so long as public order and loyalty were maintained. Christianity, however, was different—not because it was the only exclusive religion in the empire, but because it created communities that could stretch across regions and because it demanded a kind of allegiance that didn't fit neatly into traditional civic cult.

For much of the third century, Christianity remained a minority, sometimes tolerated, sometimes persecuted, often misunderstood. Under Diocletian, the empire launched what later Christians remembered as the **Great Persecution** (beginning **303**), an attempt to restore unity through religious conformity and to crush a movement seen as socially disruptive and politically suspect.

It failed.

Persecution created martyrs, and martyrs create memory. Memory hardens identity. By trying to force religious unity, the state helped forge a community that could outlast the pressure.

Then the empire pivoted—abruptly, decisively—under **Constantine**.

In **312**, Constantine fought his rival Maxentius at the **Battle of the Milvian Bridge** near Rome. He won, and within a year he and Licinius issued the **Edict of Milan (313)**, which proclaimed toleration for Christianity and restored confiscated property. Constantine's personal religious path is debated in detail—belief and politics were entangled, as they often are—but the impact is clear: Christianity moved from persecuted outsider to favored partner of imperial authority.

Constantine did not merely legalize a religion. He reimagined the relationship between heaven and empire. He patronized churches. He supported bishops as public figures. He inserted himself into theological disputes because theology now affected unity. In **325**, he convened the **Council of Nicaea**, seeking to settle disputes over the nature of Christ—questions that seem abstract until you remember that communities were splitting, riots could erupt, and imperial stability was at stake.

And then he built a new center.

In **330**, Constantine dedicated **Constantinople**, founded on the old city of Byzantium, a strategically placed capital on the Bosporus. This was not merely a new palace complex. It was a shift in gravity: toward the wealthier eastern provinces, toward defensible geography, toward the crossroads of Europe and Asia. Rome remained symbolically powerful. But the empire's most resilient heart was increasingly eastern.

A bishop's letter from this era catches the change like a photograph catches a face mid-motion. In the fourth century, bishops wrote constantly—about doctrine, about discipline, about imperial favor, about exile, about mobs, about the strange new fact that an emperor might intervene in disputes that once would have been settled locally or not settled at all. In places like Alexandria, where theological conflict could mix with urban tension, bishops became not only spiritual leaders but political actors. Letters survived because they mattered: they were tools of persuasion, pleas for protection, defenses against accusations, claims to legitimacy. A bishop could now appeal to the imperial court. He could be expelled by imperial order. He could return triumphantly when the political wind shifted. The church did not simply gain freedom. It entered power.

This was the birth of a new sacred politics: emperors presenting themselves as guardians of true faith, and bishops negotiating with imperial authority as partners, critics, and sometimes rivals.

Christianization was not a single switch flipped in 313. It was a long, uneven process. Temples did not vanish overnight. Pagan cults persisted, especially among traditional elites and in many rural regions. But the direction of state favor mattered. Endowments flowed. Church building accelerated. Christian moral language seeped into law and public ceremony. Over time, imperial authority began to lean on Christian legitimacy as a stabilizing force.

By **380**, under **Theodosius I**, the **Edict of Thessalonica** declared Nicene Christianity the empire's official faith. In subsequent years, state policy increasingly restricted certain public pagan practices, though enforcement varied. The empire that once prided itself on religious multiplicity now used religious unity as a tool of order—often with consequences it could not fully control. Because sacred politics can unify, and it can also inflame.

Urban riots did not disappear in the Christian empire. In some places, they grew more ideological, fueled by factions that could organize around theology as well as food prices. Crowds could rally behind a bishop or against one. The state could find itself facing not just "the mob," but the mob convinced it was defending truth.

Meanwhile, the empire's geography of survival was shifting. The eastern provinces—richer cities, denser tax base, strong administrative continuity—proved more capable of sustaining the costs of armies and bureaucracy. Constantinople's position and fortifications made it hard to take. The East could negotiate with frontier threats, pay subsidies, play rivals against each other, and survive crises that would have shattered a poorer state.

The West faced a harder arithmetic. By the late fourth century, pressure from migrating and confederated groups along the Danube and Rhine intensified. In **376**, Gothic groups crossed the Danube seeking refuge and entry, and mismanagement turned migration into revolt. In **378**, the Roman army suffered a devastating defeat at **Adrianople**, where Emperor **Valens** was killed. The loss signaled that the state's military dominance was no longer assured, and it forced Rome to rely more heavily on treaties, federate arrangements, and the settlement of armed groups within imperial territory.

This was not the end. It was the beginning of a new kind of imperial compromise, one that held in some regions and fractured in others.

In **410**, Visigothic forces under Alaric sacked Rome. The shock was cultural as much as strategic. Rome had been sacked before in deep history, but now it was the Christian empire's old capital, a symbol of order. The sack did not destroy the empire, but it exposed its vulnerability and deepened the sense that history had tilted.

Over the fifth century, the western empire lost key provinces and revenue sources. North Africa, a major supplier of grain and taxes, fell to the **Vandals**, who took **Carthage in 439**. Without that wealth, the Western state's ability to pay armies and maintain administration weakened further. Power in the West became increasingly localized: strongmen, generals, regional courts, bishops stepping into civic leadership as imperial structures thinned.

In **476**, the last western emperor, **Romulus Augustulus**, was deposed by **Odoacer**. The event has become a tidy textbook end date. Reality was messier. Roman law, Roman identity, and Roman institutions continued in many places. But the imperial office in the West no longer functioned as a stable center.

The East endured. The eastern Roman Empire—what later historians call Byzantium—continued to call itself Roman, continued to tax, legislate, negotiate, and fight. It faced wars, plagues, religious disputes, and immense frontier pressure. Yet it had the resources and strategic position to remain coherent when the West fragmented into successor kingdoms. Rome, then, did not "fall" in one moment. It transformed.

The third-century crisis forced the state to change its bones: more bureaucracy, more fiscal extraction, a more militarized economy, a heavier hand in daily life. Constantine and his successors changed its soul-language: sacred authority fused with imperial authority, Christianity moved into the center of public legitimacy, bishops became state-level actors. The West, with weaker revenues and harsher frontier dynamics, broke into new political forms. The East, with stronger urban wealth and a new capital, remained resilient.

Return to the frontier soldier. Years after that riot in Rome, after reforms and new capitals and new gods favored by emperors, he still waits at the edge, still listens to the wind over trees or steppe grass, still counts his pay and measures its worth. He has learned to live inside a state that demands more and promises more, that prays differently than his ancestors did, that speaks of salvation alongside taxes.

And somewhere in a city, a bishop seals a letter, sending it along the same roads that carry soldiers and grain. Somewhere else, a crowd gathers, not only hungry now but certain—certain that God, justice, and the emperor ought to agree, and furious when they do not.

29

Lords of the Middle Corridor

The envoy's horse is lathered when he reaches the river. On the western bank, Roman soldiers stand in a line that looks casual until you notice the way their hands stay close to their belts. On the eastern bank, Persian guards do not shift at all; they simply watch, faces still, eyes narrowed against the light. Between them the water moves steadily, carrying reeds and the occasional broken branch, indifferent to banners.

The envoy dismounts and waits while a clerk checks seals—wax on one side, clay on the other—because in this world a war can start from a forged letter as easily as from a raiding party. He carries gifts that are also signals: fine cloth, perhaps, and silver; words that have been rehearsed until they sound natural; and a promise that is never simply a promise. He is here to negotiate a frontier that is less a line than a living seam. Towns on it speak multiple languages. Merchants cross it with permits and bribes. Soldiers cross it with torches.

This is the middle corridor of late antiquity: the stretch of land and desert routes, river crossings and mountain passes between the Mediterranean world and the deep interior of Asia. Rome sits on one end of it. Iran sits on the other—anchoring, regulating, profiting, and fighting for it.

If Rome in the third and fourth centuries learned to survive by thickening its bureaucracy and fusing itself to a new sacred politics, Iran was doing something similar on the opposite side of the frontier. And the rivalry between the two was not a side plot. It was one of the main ways the late ancient world was organized: two imperial systems facing each other across Mesopotamia and Armenia, trading blows and treaties, fortifying borders, and competing to control the routes that carried silk, spices, and the rumors of distant powers.

To see how this rivalry took shape, you have to begin with a transformation inside Iran itself.

For centuries before late antiquity, the **Parthian** Arsacid dynasty had ruled much of Iran and Mesopotamia (traditionally dated from the mid-third century BCE to the early third century CE). Parthian power had a particular texture: not a rigid centralized machine like later empires tried to be, but a great confederated realm where noble houses held enormous influence, and kings ruled partly by negotiation with aristocratic elites. Parthian armies were famous for horse archers and armored cavalry, and Parthian rule sat astride the east–west routes that made the empire wealthy.

Rome learned early that this was not a frontier to treat lightly. The defeat of Crassus at **Carrhae (53 BCE)** had already shown what Parthian mobility and archery could do to a heavy Roman force. Even when Rome won victories, it struggled to make them permanent in the east. Distance and supply lines mattered. So did local loyalties. So did the reality that Mesopotamia was not a blank space to be "held," but a dense landscape of cities, canals, and communities with their own stakes.

By the early third century CE, however, the Parthian system was vulnerable—strained by internal rivalries and the pressure of managing a huge realm with a comparatively loose central grip. Into that moment rose a new power from the southwest Iranian region of Persis: **Ardashir**, who defeated the last Parthian king, **Artabanus IV**, around **224 CE**. Ardashir's victory is often treated as a dynastic change, but it was more than that. It was a new claim about what kingship should be.

The new dynasty called itself **Sasanian**, and it presented itself as the restorer of a more ancient Persian order, drawing legitimacy from memory and religion. Whether or not that claim was "true" in a simple sense is less important than the political effect: the Sasanians framed their rule as divinely sanctioned and culturally central, not merely one noble house among others. They tightened administration, strengthened the monarchy's ideological aura, and made the empire feel more like a single system with a single center.

That center was the great urban complex around **Ctesiphon** on the Tigris—an imperial seat facing Rome's eastern provinces across a frontier that would become one of the most heavily contested zones on earth.

The wars began almost immediately. Ardashir pressed into Roman territory; his son **Shapur I** pushed harder. In the mid-third century, while Rome was buckling under the crisis of rapid imperial turnover and frontier assaults, Shapur fought a sequence of campaigns that culminated in one of the most humiliating moments in Roman imperial history: in **260 CE**, Emperor **Valerian** was captured by the Persians. Ancient accounts surround the event with propaganda and later storytelling, but the core fact remains: Rome's emperor became a prisoner of Iran.

The capture mattered far beyond a battlefield. It told every border city, every allied king, every wavering governor that Rome could bleed and stumble—and that the Sasanian state was not a peripheral power, but an imperial rival with the capacity to break Roman prestige.

Yet the story is not one of Iran simply rising while Rome falls. Both empires were wounded giants learning how to endure.

Rome responded by reforming, militarizing, and reorganizing under emperors like Diocletian and Constantine. The Sasanians, for their part, built a state that could sustain long wars—because sustained war is expensive, and expense requires administration, and administration requires legitimacy.

This is where the frontier becomes the real protagonist. The Rome–Iran border was not a wall in the modern imagination. It was a zone of forts, watchtowers, and fortified cities; of contested client kingdoms; of strategic river crossings and mountain passes; of agriculture and taxation; of people who lived with the constant possibility that a campaign season could ruin them.

Mesopotamia was the hinge. Cities like **Nisibis** and **Edessa** and later **Dara** could become the focus of imperial attention precisely because they were not just towns—they were keys. Control a fortified city and you control roads, granaries, and the movement of armies. Lose one and the frontier shifts. Even when treaties fixed borders, the fixedness was fragile, because each side knew that next year's emperor might want a different line.

In **298 CE**, after war between Rome and the Sasanian king **Narseh**, the Romans under Diocletian's regime secured a favorable treaty that strengthened Rome's position in the east for a time. But such treaties were not final settlements. They were pauses shaped by exhaustion and opportunity. The corridor did not stop being valuable because a treaty was signed. It became even more valuable, because now both empires had time to build, stock, and plan for the next turn.

By the fourth century, the rivalry took on a sharper religious edge.

The Sasanians were deeply tied to **Zoroastrian** traditions, and over time Zoroastrian institutions and priestly authority became more closely linked to the state. The relationship was not always simple—religion is never a single lever pulled by a king—but the imperial presentation mattered. When a ruler claims to uphold cosmic order, political loyalty becomes sacred duty, and dissent can be framed as more than rebellion.

You can feel that sacred dimension in a fire temple. A flame burns behind a screen, not flickering like a household hearth but maintained with a kind of disciplined care, fed, guarded from impurity, treated as a living symbol of order. The temple air carries the smell of ash and resin. Priests move with practiced restraint. People come not only to ask for blessings but to locate themselves in a moral universe where truth and falsehood are not opinions but forces.

In late antiquity, this mattered because the empire was a tapestry of religions:

Zoroastrians, Jews, Christians, Manichaeans, and many others. The state could not ignore these communities because belief was social infrastructure. It shaped loyalties, networks, and the willingness of people to accept imperial demands.

Christianity, in particular, became politically charged after Constantine favored it in the Roman world. To a Sasanian ruler watching from Ctesiphon, Christians inside Iran could look like a potential fifth column—not because every Christian was disloyal, but because religion now crossed imperial borders with a new intensity. Under **Shapur II** (reigned **309–379 CE**), when Rome and Iran fought long wars, Christian communities in Iran faced suspicion and, at times, persecution. The logic was cruelly practical: if Rome's emperor is now the patron of Christians, then Christians in Iran become politically ambiguous in the eyes of a state obsessed with security.

And yet, the Sasanian system also knew how to use religious policy pragmatically. Tolerance and repression could both be tools depending on context, local politics, and external threats. Kings needed the support of elites and priests, but they also needed tax revenue and stability. A policy that provoked widespread unrest could be as dangerous as a foreign army.

The rivalry was not only westward. Iran's "middle corridor" position meant it was also exposed to the vast steppe world to the north and northeast. In late antiquity, pressure from nomadic and semi-nomadic confederations—often labeled in sources as "Huns," and later including powerful groups like the **Hephthalites** (White Huns)—forced the Sasanians to fight on multiple fronts. This is one reason frontier fortifications became such a feature of the empire's imagination. When you live between worlds, you fortify the doors.

In the Caucasus, passes and coastal gates mattered because they were points where steppe raiders could pour in. Fortification projects associated with places like **Derbent** (the "Caspian Gates") reflect the strategic obsession with sealing vulnerabilities. Further east, massive defensive lines such as the **Wall of Gorgan** (often dated to the late Sasanian era by many scholars, though precise dating debates exist) show the same impulse at a different scale: build barriers where open terrain invites fast-moving enemies.

These walls were not magical shields. They were tools to slow, channel, and signal—forcing movement into predictable routes where garrisons could respond. Fortifications bought time, and time is often what saves an empire. But the Sasanians did not merely defend. They competed.

In **363 CE**, Emperor **Julian** launched a major campaign against Persia and died during the retreat—another reminder that the east could swallow Roman ambition. In the fifth and sixth centuries, the pattern continued: wars, truces, border skirmishes, and negotiations. Sometimes the conflict hinged on client regions like **Armenia**, a land of mountains and loyalties where choosing a side could be a matter of survival. Sometimes it hinged on a single fortress city. Sometimes it hinged on money.

Because rivalry at this level is always partly financial. Here is the part of the story that looks boring until you realize it can move armies: **silk taxes**.

Silk was not "just cloth." It was prestige compressed into fabric—light enough to transport, valuable enough to finance diplomacy, desirable enough to make emperors care about distant routes. Chinese silk reached the Mediterranean through a chain of intermediaries and corridors: Central Asian merchants, steppe routes, oasis towns, and the states that controlled the bottlenecks.

Iran sat on the crucial middle stretches of that chain. That meant leverage.

Picture a customs station near an oasis, or a river crossing where caravan routes converge. A clerk sits with scales and seals. Bales are opened just enough to prove what they are. A tax is assessed. Not always in coin—sometimes in goods, sometimes in negotiated "gifts" that are taxes by another name. The merchant pays because refusal is not heroic; refusal is ruin. The state takes its share because the corridor's value is one of the empire's main strategic advantages.

This is how Iran could pressure Rome without always fighting it. If you can influence the price and flow of luxury goods, you can influence elites, diplomacy, even the fiscal balance of your rival. Rome could try to bypass Persian control through Red Sea routes and Indian Ocean trade, and it did. But the overland corridors remained politically potent, and the Sasanians knew it. The rivalry, then, was not simply two armies meeting at a border. It was two systems competing to control chokepoints in a connected world: Mesopotamian fortress lines, Armenian highlands, Caucasus passes, oasis cities, and the corridors that linked the Mediterranean to Central Asia and beyond. Inside the Sasanian realm, this competition shaped the state's internal life.

A court that must fund constant readiness needs reliable extraction. That pushes administrative development: land assessments, tax organization, labor obligations, and a social order that can supply cavalry and infantry. The Sasanians cultivated an elite warrior class, supported by landed wealth and tied to the monarchy. They also maintained urban centers and craft production, because empires do not fight with swords alone; they fight with supplies.

In the late fifth and early sixth centuries, the strain of maintaining order and funding war contributed to internal turbulence, including reformist religious-social movements like **Mazdakism**, associated with **Mazdak** and the reign of **Kavad I** (late fifth to early sixth century). Sources—often hostile—portray the movement as calling for social leveling and communal sharing in ways that threatened elites. Whatever the exact doctrines, the political meaning is clear: when inequality hardens and the burdens of empire intensify, moral critique can become a political force.

The response, particularly under **Khosrow I (Anushirvan)** (reigned **531–579 CE**), is remembered as a period of consolidation and reform—administrative strengthening, fiscal reorganization, and a renewed emphasis on imperial order. Khosrow also fought Rome (now the eastern Roman Empire centered on Constantinople) and managed frontier threats while cultivating an image of wise kingship. In late antiquity, "wisdom" is often the language empires use when they want to make power look stable.

Meanwhile, Rome's eastern half—the empire that would later be called Byzantium—was learning the same lesson: survival required administrative strength, ideological cohesion, and careful frontier management. It built fortifications too. It founded and fortified cities like **Dara** near the Persian frontier in the early sixth century, precisely because the border was not calming down; it was becoming a permanent strategic equation.

So what did the Iran–Rome rivalry do to the world between 200 and 600 CE?

It militarized it. Borderlands became garrison landscapes. Cities became walls with markets attached. Rural communities learned to endure requisitions and raids. Fortifications reshaped movement.

It bureaucratized it. Both sides developed deeper administrative systems to fund and supply war. Tax structures and state control thickened.

It spiritualized it. Legitimacy drew more heavily on religious language, and religious communities became entangled with politics—sometimes protected, sometimes persecuted, always watched.

And it connected it. War did not stop trade. In many ways it organized trade, forcing merchants into safer corridors, elevating intermediaries, and making chokepoints more valuable. The "middle corridor" remained a conduit for goods and ideas precisely because so many states fought to control it.

Return to the envoy at the river. He finally crosses, escorted, eyes forward. He delivers his message in a fortress hall where banners hang and officials listen without revealing anything on their faces. The words are polite; the meanings are sharp. There will be a tribute payment, or there will be a campaign. There will be prisoners exchanged, or there will be a raid. There will be a treaty line, or there will be a siege.

Outside, the frontier city continues its ordinary life: bakers, smiths, children carrying water, merchants arguing in multiple tongues.

People marry across cultures. Soldiers gamble. Priests keep their rituals. The empire's great rivalry is lived as daily uncertainty.

In a fire temple, the flame keeps burning, guarded against impurity, a symbol of order in a world where borders are never fully secure.

At a customs station, silk bales are weighed, and the state takes its portion—because even in an age of saints and emperors, nothing moves without someone profiting.

30

The Golden Age Puzzle

The copper plate is warm from the hands that have carried it through the crowd. In the temple courtyard the air smells of clarified butter and crushed marigold. A bell rings once, then again, a sound that seems to hang in the stone. The plate is not large, but it has been polished until it catches light. Lines of carefully cut letters march across it in a script meant to outlast the donor's breath. This is not a private gift slipped into a priest's palm. It is a public act, witnessed and recorded: land granted, boundaries named, taxes remitted, a share of harvest promised in perpetuity.

A grant like this is a kind of architecture. It builds a relationship between ruler, ritual, and countryside. It turns fields into revenue and revenue into legitimacy. It also turns language into power. The inscription is in **Sanskrit**, the learned tongue increasingly favored in royal claims and religious foundations across much of South Asia.

The donor's name matters. The temple's god matters. The village names matter. But what matters most is the confidence beneath it all: the belief that a cultural world can be made coherent across distance, that people who will never meet can still share a vocabulary of law, devotion, and prestige.

This is the "cosmopolis" of South Asia's classical age: not a single empire that rules everything, but a broad zone where culture, language, and trade begin to knit elites, institutions, and religious life into recognizable patterns from the Hindu Kush to the Bay of Bengal, and outward across the sea toward Southeast Asia.

It does not arrive in one year. It grows in layers, through conquest and commerce, through monasteries and courts, through ships that leave on the right wind and return with more than goods in their holds.

After the Mauryan unification and its moral experiment under Ashoka, the subcontinent did not remain one political unit. Power fractured, then regrouped in different regions. Yet the fragmentation did not mean isolation. In many ways it meant the opposite. Multiple courts competed for prestige. Multiple routes competed for commerce. Multiple religious institutions competed for patronage. The result was a world thick with movement and rivalry, where being connected became an advantage you could tax, display, and convert into authority.

In the northwest, connection took a particularly dramatic form under the **Kushans**.

The Kushans emerged from the **Yuezhi**, groups who had moved into Bactria and the region around the Oxus after upheavals on the steppe. By the **first century CE**, Kushan rulers controlled territory that spanned what is now parts of Afghanistan, Pakistan, and northern India, bridging Central Asia and the Gangetic world. Their power sat directly on the routes that carried silk, horses, precious stones, and ideas between the Han frontiers, Iranian lands, and the northern subcontinent.

A Kushan king did not need to claim to be "Indian" or "Greek" or "Persian" in a pure sense. The very strength of the Kushan realm was its mixed inheritance. Coins and art from the period show a remarkable cultural range: Hellenistic styles alongside Iranian motifs, local Indian religious imagery alongside royal iconography designed for a multi-ethnic empire. This was not confusion. It was strategy. A ruler who can speak in multiple symbolic languages can rule multiple audiences.

The most famous Kushan monarch, **Kanishka I** (commonly placed in the second century CE, though exact dating is debated), is often linked to a surge in Buddhist patronage. Under Kushan power, Buddhism did not remain only a monastic path for renunciants. It became an institution that could operate across long distances: monasteries along trade routes, networks of teachers and pilgrims, donors who offered wealth for merit, rulers who supported monasteries because monasteries stabilized movement and signaled moral legitimacy.

Along the northwest frontier, the Buddhist world took on new artistic forms that still shape how the Buddha is imagined today. In regions such as **Gandhara**, artists produced images of the Buddha in human form with stylistic influences that suggest a long contact zone: draped garments, carved folds, a visual language that could feel familiar to travelers from far away. Whether every stylistic feature is directly "Greek" is less important than the broader truth: the Kushan realm helped make Buddhism visually portable. A faith with a recognizable icon can travel faster, because recognition builds community.

Kushan power also drew wealth from trade. When caravans moved through the passes and plains, someone taxed them. When markets grew in cities like **Mathura**, crafts and commerce created patrons eager to fund monuments, sculptures, and temples. The Kushans did not invent long-distance exchange, but they sat astride it at a moment when Eurasian routes were thickening, and they profited by making themselves indispensable.

This mattered for South Asia's "classical age" because it laid down a pattern that would repeat: political power leveraging movement, and religious-cultural institutions growing alongside commerce.

Further east, another dynasty would shape the classical image of India even more strongly: the **Guptas**.

The Gupta rise is usually dated to the early fourth century CE, with **Chandragupta I** beginning a new era of power around **320 CE**, and the dynasty reaching impressive strength under rulers such as **Samudragupta** (mid-fourth century) and **Chandragupta II** (late fourth to early fifth century). The Guptas did not rule the entire subcontinent. Their core strength lay in northern India, and their influence varied by region and time. Yet their court culture became unusually influential, partly because it was strategically cultivated, and partly because it arrived at a moment when Sanskrit and Brahmanical institutions were becoming powerful vehicles for legitimacy.

Walk into a Gupta court, and you can feel how rule becomes performance. The hall is not only a place where decisions are made. It is a stage where authority is announced through ritual, generosity, and learning. Officials stand in ordered ranks. Petitioners wait with gifts that are also evidence of loyalty. A recitation begins, and the cadence of Sanskrit, formal and controlled, carries a kind of gravity that local tongues might not be allowed to claim in that setting. A court does not merely govern. It declares what counts as refined, lawful, and worthy.

A scholar at such a court is not just an ornament. He is a tool of statecraft. He composes genealogies that tie a ruling line to heroic pasts. He praises victories in a language meant to be read beyond one region. He codifies ideals of kingship: the ruler as protector, giver, upholder of order. Inscriptions from this era often speak in that tone, and their very existence hints at a crucial shift. A king wants his deeds remembered not only by local memory but by a wider literate culture. The court language becomes a bridge across distance, allowing a ruler's claim to travel in stone and copper.

This is one reason the term **Sanskritization** is so useful, as long as it's handled carefully. It does not mean the subcontinent became culturally uniform. It means that Sanskrit, Brahmanical ritual forms, and certain models of social hierarchy became widely adopted as prestige tools by many groups, including those not originally at the core of Brahmanical tradition.

Local elites could sponsor temples, invite Brahmins, commission genealogies, and adopt Sanskrit titles to make their authority look ancient and rightful. Kings could issue land grants that tied religious specialists to the countryside, anchoring loyalty and building institutions that outlived individual reigns. Villages could find themselves linked to temples and monasteries through obligations that were both spiritual and economic. The process created cohesion, but it also created exclusions. A "classical" culture can be beautiful and disciplined, and also deeply unequal in whose voice it amplifies.

Religion in this era did not move in a single direction. It branched and competed. Buddhism remained strong and diverse. The forms often grouped under **Mahayana** Buddhism expanded, emphasizing new scriptures, new devotional practices, and a broader cosmos of bodhisattvas. Monastic institutions did not only preserve doctrine; they became economic actors—landholders, educators, patrons of art, hosts to travelers. Great centers of learning would later become famous, and while the exact origins of specific institutions are debated, the broad trend is clear: education and religion increasingly formed durable networks that could stretch across regions.

At the same time, what we now call **Hinduism** was taking on more recognizable shapes through the growth of devotional cults, temple institutions, and a vast body of narrative and ritual literature often labeled "Puranic." Older Vedic sacrificial traditions did not vanish, but the center of gravity shifted toward gods and goddesses whose worship could be expressed in temple ritual and personal devotion. **Vishnu**, **Shiva**, and powerful goddess traditions gained prominence, not as abstract concepts, but as living centers of community life. Devotion was not only private feeling. It became a public practice supported by endowments, festivals, and local economies.

This is where the temple donation from the opening scene fits into a wider logic. A temple is not only a spiritual building. It is an employer. It is a landholder. It is a calendar-maker. It organizes artisans, priests, musicians, and the flow of food and wealth. When rulers sponsor temples, they are sponsoring social infrastructure. They are also tying holiness to the state's claim that order is being upheld.

And the "classical" label so often attached to the Gupta era is not just about art and literature, though those mattered. It is also about administration and economy.

The Gupta state relied on systems of revenue and local governance that varied across regions. There were officials, land grants, and a relationship between center and local powers that could be flexible rather than uniformly centralized. In many places, local elites and regional rulers played decisive roles, operating within a cultural framework that could still recognize Gupta supremacy or Gupta prestige. This kind of layered rule can look weaker than a rigid bureaucracy, but it can also be resilient, because it allows adaptation to diverse landscapes and local politics.

Meanwhile, trade continued to bind South Asia to wider worlds. Overland routes remained important, especially in the northwest, connecting through Iranian lands and Central Asia into broader Eurasian exchange. But maritime trade was becoming ever more central to South Asia's cosmopolitan reach, because the sea could carry bulk goods and luxury goods in rhythms that were seasonal but reliable.

Here the ship captain's log becomes the most honest form of history. He does not write poetry. He records timing, cargo, hazards. He notes when the winds turn and when they fail. He lists what is loaded: textiles, beads, perhaps spices and aromatics, perhaps metal goods and finished crafts. He marks water supplies. He keeps track of the crew. He notes where the ship will make landfall, because ports are not just geography, they are politics. You need permission, protection, and reliable brokers.

The monsoon makes this world possible. Sailors who understand it can leave India's coasts and cross to Sri Lanka, to the Arabian Sea, to the Bay of Bengal, and onward toward the shores of Southeast Asia. They do not sail into emptiness. They sail between nodes: ports where merchants gather, where customs are assessed, where diasporic communities offer trust, where local rulers cultivate revenue by protecting trade.

This is how South Asia's cultural influence traveled to Southeast Asia, and it is crucial to understand what that influence was and wasn't. It was not a simple story of Indian conquest or mass settlement remaking the region from the outside. It was a story of exchange and selective adoption, mediated by trade, marriage alliances, religious specialists, and the desires of Southeast Asian elites to build legitimacy in a connected world.

In early Southeast Asian polities such as **Funan** (active in the early centuries CE) and later emerging kingdoms along the coasts and river deltas, rulers began to use Sanskrit titles, commission Sanskrit inscriptions, and adopt forms of court ritual and religious architecture that linked them into a prestigious wider sphere. These were local states making strategic choices. Sanskrit was useful because it carried an aura of learning and sacred authority. Brahmanical and Buddhist practices were useful because they offered models of kingship, cosmic order, and merit. Temple building was useful because it anchored power in stone and ritual. Trade was useful because it funded all of it.

The result was a maritime-connected cultural zone that stretched from South Asia into the Bay of Bengal and beyond, a cosmopolis not of one language spoken by everyone, but of shared symbols among elites, institutions, and religious communities. A traveler could move from port to port and find familiar signs: a shrine form, a ritual calendar, a script style, a title, a story about a god or a righteous king. This was cohesion, but it was also tension.

As Sanskritized court culture spread, it could elevate some groups and marginalize others. As temples accumulated land and wealth, they could become sources of local conflict as well as local pride. As Buddhist and Hindu institutions competed for patronage, theological debates and institutional rivalries shaped what was taught, built, and remembered. As trade intensified, coastal regions could prosper while inland communities bore heavier extraction burdens to fund states and religious endowments. Cosmopolitanism is never evenly shared. It is an advantage that concentrates, then radiates outward in diluted forms.

Still, something important had happened by the time we reach the fifth and sixth centuries CE. South Asia had become not just a region of kingdoms, but a generator of cultural templates that traveled with merchants and monks. It had created a durable learned language for prestige and governance. It had expanded religious institutions capable of operating across distance. It had participated in trade systems that linked the Mediterranean and Iranian corridors on one side and Southeast Asia on the other.

Return to the copper plate in the temple courtyard. It will be buried in a foundation deposit or stored carefully, consulted in disputes, read aloud to confirm rights. A century later, someone might trace the letters with a finger to prove the grant still stands. Another century later, the dynasty might be gone, and the grant might still be invoked, because institutions often outlive kings.

In the court, the scholar finishes a text meant to praise a ruler, but it also praises a world: a world where language can unify prestige, where ritual can anchor authority, where learning can become a political tool. On the coast, the ship captain waits for the right wind again. The monsoon does not care about dynasties. It turns, reliably, and in turning it carries the cosmopolis outward.

31

Empire Reassembled

In the monastery courtyard, the day begins before the sun has fully warmed the tiles. A bell sounds once, clean and spare. A thin mist clings to the cypress branches. Inside a hall that smells of lamp oil and ink, a novice kneels at a low table with a brush poised above paper. The characters he copies have traveled farther than any soldier in this region ever will. They came by caravan and ship, through ports and passes, carried by merchants, monks, and diplomats. They speak of suffering and release, of compassion and discipline, of worlds layered like veils.

Outside the walls, the road is still dangerous. Bandits move in the hills when taxes fail and armies pass through. Refugees drift south with whatever they can carry. A local official's authority shrinks to the distance his messengers can ride in one day. And yet here, behind temple gates, the work continues. Line after line. Sutra after sutra. A different kind of infrastructure is being built: not walls or roads, but a shared language of meaning that can survive the collapse of dynasties.

This is what China's long age of disunion feels like when you stand inside it. The empire that the Han once held together fractures, but life does not stop. It rearranges. New elites form. New frontiers harden. New faiths find room to grow. And when reunification finally comes, it does not arrive as a return to an old order. It arrives as a rebuild, using tools forged in the very centuries of division that seemed, at first glance, like only loss.

The story begins with an ending.

The **Han dynasty**, which had built a durable bureaucratic model and pushed its influence outward, entered crisis in the late second century CE. The reasons were multiple and mutually reinforcing: factional court politics, local magnates accumulating power, fiscal strain, and the grinding pressure of rebellion and frontier insecurity. In **184 CE**, the **Yellow Turban** uprising erupted, one of several major disturbances that revealed how brittle the state had become at ground level. Even when the rebellion was suppressed, it left behind a landscape where generals and regional strongmen held real power, often more real than imperial decrees.

By **220 CE**, the last Han emperor was forced to abdicate, and the political world splintered into the era later known as the **Three Kingdoms**: **Wei** in the north, **Shu** in the southwest, and **Wu** in the southeast. The names sound neat; the reality was violent. War became the default grammar of politics. The center could not hold because there was no longer a center strong enough to make others obey.

The Three Kingdoms period (commonly dated **220–280 CE**) is remembered in later literature as a heroic age of strategy and loyalty. The historical core is harsher. It was an era of competing states trying to extract resources from exhausted populations, fighting for territory, talent, and legitimacy. Armies marched and requisitioned. Local communities fortified themselves. Refugees moved toward safer zones. Administrators learned to govern under permanent strain.

A brief reunification came under the **Jin dynasty**, which conquered Wu in **280 CE** and restored a single imperial court. But the reunification did not last. Internal conflict among elite factions and princes weakened the dynasty, and pressure from the north intensified. By **316 CE**, after major upheavals and invasions, the Western Jin had collapsed.

What followed was not simply "chaos." It was a new political ecology.

In the north, a sequence of regimes rose and fell in a period later called the **Sixteen Kingdoms** (a label that simplifies a complex reality). Many were founded by groups that Chinese sources often described as "barbarian," but those categories were political and cultural judgments as much as ethnography. The important fact is that northern China became a frontier zone where steppe and settled worlds collided and fused: cavalry warfare, confederated leadership, and rapid mobility meeting walled cities, tax registers, and bureaucratic routines.

In the south, the Jin court re-established itself across the Yangtze, creating what historians call the **Eastern Jin**. Over the centuries that followed, southern China saw a sequence of dynasties—**Liu Song, Southern Qi, Liang, Chen**—

often grouped as the **Southern Dynasties**. Meanwhile, the north eventually consolidated under stronger regimes, most notably the **Northern Wei**, founded by the **Tuoba Xianbei**, which unified much of northern China by **439 CE**.

From roughly the **fourth to the late sixth century CE**, China existed as a divided world: northern courts with deep steppe interactions and militarized frontiers, and southern courts shaped by migration, gentry culture, and a different balance of agriculture and commerce. This was the era of the **Northern and Southern Dynasties** (often dated **420–589 CE**, though the transition into it is gradual).

Disunity did not freeze history. It accelerated certain changes. One of the most visible changes was demographic and cultural: a massive movement of people southward. Waves of refugees, officials, and elite families crossed the Yangtze over decades, sometimes in organized transfers, sometimes in panicked flight. They brought with them northern styles of governance and elite culture, but they also adapted to the south's landscapes and economies. The south's wetlands and river systems could be extraordinarily productive, and as settlement intensified, southern regions grew in importance. Over time, the "south" stopped being a periphery and became a rival heartland with its own courts, its own aristocracies, and its own self-confidence.

You can feel that shift in the life of a refugee family. A small boat hugs the riverbank, moving through gray water with slow urgency. The family's goods are packed into bundles tied with rope. Some items are practical: tools, cooking pots, seed grain. Some are symbols: a seal that proves an office held under the old regime, a few books wrapped in cloth, an ancestor tablet carried carefully as if it were a living person. The parents look over their shoulders too often. A rumor travels faster than boats: a fort has fallen, a commander has switched sides, a tax collector has become a bandit.

They are not leaving because they want novelty. They are leaving because the north is becoming a place where tomorrow cannot be predicted. The south is not safety. It is only a different set of risks.

On the far bank, a new world begins. Land is available, but it is contested. Local families hold influence. Disease patterns are different. The language of power is familiar, but the people who speak it are not. Refugees must bargain for protection and legitimacy, sometimes marrying into southern lineages, sometimes building new enclaves, sometimes living for generations with the memory of "home" as a story told at meals.

Over time, these movements helped create new elites. In the south, powerful aristocratic clans dominated offices and culture, shaping court life and administration. In the north, ruling houses often had to balance steppe military traditions with the practical demands of governing dense agricultural populations. The result, on both sides, was an intensified focus on institutions: land control, taxation, military recruitment, and legitimacy narratives strong enough to hold diverse populations.

Steppe interactions were not merely raids and invasions. They were structural.

Northern regimes depended heavily on cavalry and mobile warfare, which shaped military organization and frontier strategy. At the same time, ruling in northern China required more than mobility. It required grain, labor, and records. This pushed steppe-origin elites to adopt, adapt, and sometimes reshape Chinese administrative practices. The Northern Wei, for example, developed increasingly sophisticated governance and pursued policies that aimed to stabilize revenue and control the countryside. Scholars debate details and motivations, but the broad trajectory is clear: in a divided world, survival rewarded states that could combine military strength with administrative depth.

This is one of the great ironies of the period. The very forces often portrayed as "outside" China helped produce political tools that later "Chinese" empires would inherit.

If politics was fragmented, ideology was searching. This is where Buddhism's spread becomes one of the defining transformations of the era. Buddhism had entered China earlier, likely through a mix of overland and maritime routes in the first centuries CE, but it was during the centuries of disunion that it became deeply rooted across social levels and regions. Part of the reason is painfully simple: Buddhism spoke to suffering in a world where suffering was widespread.

It offered a moral vocabulary that did not depend on the stability of one dynasty. It offered practices—ritual, chanting, meditation, monastic discipline—that could be carried from place to place. It offered institutions—monasteries—that could provide food, shelter, and community. It offered legitimacy to rulers who needed a sacred language that could transcend local lineages. And it offered hope to commoners whose lives were being rewritten by war and forced movement.

In the monastery, that hope becomes daily routine. Monks rise, eat sparingly, and work. They copy texts. They teach. They host travelers who arrive with dust on their clothes and fear in their eyes. Some monasteries become wealthy through patronage and land. Some become entangled with court politics. Some are simple refuges. The monastic network becomes a parallel infrastructure: not replacing the state, but surviving its instability and sometimes stabilizing it.

Buddhism also forced Chinese thinkers to argue anew about the nature of the self, ethics, and authority. Translators struggled to render Indian concepts into Chinese vocabulary, and their choices reshaped both. Debates emerged about emptiness, compassion, karma, and salvation. For elites, Buddhism could be a philosophy and a practice. For rulers, it could be a source of legitimacy and merit. For ordinary people, it could be a ritual language for grief, illness, and hope.

This did not mean older traditions vanished. Confucian norms still shaped administration and family life. Daoist practices and texts continued to evolve. But the presence of Buddhism widened the spiritual marketplace, and in a divided political world, that spiritual competition mattered.

Meanwhile, the division between north and south created different cultural tones.

Southern courts developed a refined aristocratic culture, with literary salons and courtly aesthetics, shaped partly by the confidence of elites who saw themselves as guardians of "true" Chinese tradition after losing the north. Northern courts, facing constant frontier pressure, often emphasized military readiness and pragmatic governance, while also sponsoring grand religious projects that asserted universal kingship. Across both, culture became a way to claim legitimacy when bloodlines and borders were unstable.

So why, after centuries of division, did reunification become possible again?

Because disunity incubated the tools of unity. The north developed militarized states capable of large-scale mobilization. Administrative systems deepened because war and governance demanded it. The south developed economic strength and population density that no reunifying power could ignore. Religious institutions created networks of influence that rulers could harness. Roads, canals, and tax systems became ever more crucial as states tried to feed armies and cities. By the late sixth century, the map looked fragmented, but the underlying political technologies were mature.

Into that landscape stepped the **Sui**.

In **581 CE**, **Yang Jian** seized power in the north and founded the Sui dynasty (as **Emperor Wen**). He inherited northern military strength and administrative experience, and he used them with a clear goal: reunify China. In **589 CE**, Sui forces conquered the southern Chen dynasty, ending the centuries-long political division in a formal sense.

Reunification required more than victories. It required rebuilding the arteries of the state. This is where the official rebuilding roads becomes the clearest image of the Sui project.

An engineer-official stands at a muddy cut where a road has collapsed into a ditch. He is not a poet. He is a man with measurements and deadlines. He inspects the earth, orders labor gangs to dig and tamp, assigns timber for a bridge, and checks supply stations that will feed workers and future travelers. Behind him are ledgers and quotas. Ahead of him is an empire that can only exist if movement is reliable.

The Sui rebuilt and expanded infrastructure precisely because a reunified realm needs circulation: grain moving to capitals and garrisons, officials traveling to provinces, taxes reaching the center, armies redeploying quickly when frontiers flare. The most famous project associated with the Sui is the expansion of the **Grand Canal** system, linking northern and southern waterways. Later dynasties, especially the Tang and Song, would benefit enormously from this integration. The canal is not just engineering. It is politics in water form: a way to tie regional economies into one state.

Sui governance also drew on the administrative lessons of the period: centralized authority, standardized systems, and the cultivation of officials. The groundwork for later examination systems was strengthened in this era, though the full maturation came later. What matters is the direction: a state trying to make competence and control scalable again, to turn the chaos of disunion into a unified administrative rhythm.

The Sui did not last long (it fell in **618 CE**), in part because the same projects that made reunification possible also created strain: heavy labor demands, ambitious campaigns, and the ever-present danger that a state will overreach before legitimacy has settled. But even the Sui's short reign mattered because it proved reunification could be done and left behind the connective infrastructure and administrative habits that the **Tang** would inherit and expand.

Return to the monastery where we began. The sutras copied in the early morning are not erased by reunification. If anything, they become more important. Buddhism, now deeply rooted, will continue to shape Chinese society, politics, art, and international connections. The refugee family's descendants, settled in the south, are no longer refugees; they are locals with layered ancestry and memories that have become family legend. The official's rebuilt roads carry not only soldiers and tax grain, but pilgrims, merchants, monks, and ideas.

China's division was not a pause between empires. It was a forge. It forged new elites and new institutions, hardened frontiers and deepened administrations, and widened the spiritual and cultural horizons of what it meant to live in a Chinese world. When unity returned, it returned not as a restoration of the Han, but as a new synthesis built from centuries of fracture.

32

Africa Unbound

In the river town the air is thick with heat and voices. Canoes nudge the muddy bank, their hulls scuffed from long travel. People step out with bundles balanced on heads or tied to shoulders—salt wrapped in cloth, dried fish, gourds of oil, woven mats, bars of iron that ring faintly when they knock together. A woman squats beside a basket of kola nuts and fans away flies. A man holds up a length of cloth and argues about its quality with someone who answers in a different tongue. Children thread through legs and loads like water through reeds.

Nothing here looks like an empire in the Roman sense. There is no marble forum, no legionary standard. Yet this market is a node in something just as decisive: the growth of African networks across deserts, rivers, and coasts—systems that link people who will never meet, moving goods, technologies, and beliefs along routes shaped by ecology and ingenuity.

If the classical age taught us that roads and sea lanes can turn distance into routine, late antiquity and the early medieval centuries show the same lesson in African form. Between roughly **200 and 600 CE**—and continuing beyond—Africa's internal connections deepened and its external ties multiplied. States rose where chokepoints could be controlled. Towns grew where rivers made exchange efficient. Iron spread as both tool and weapon. And along the Indian Ocean littoral, coastal communities began to turn the sea itself into a marketplace, marked by beads that could travel farther than any king's shout.

Begin in the northeast, where highlands and sea routes make power possible: **Aksum**.

By the first centuries CE, Aksum had become a state with reach that stretched from the Ethiopian/Eritrean highlands down to the Red Sea. Its strength came from a combination that seems almost designed for durability: productive agriculture in the highlands, control over routes to the coast, and participation in the Red Sea–Indian Ocean trading system. Aksumite rulers minted coins and carved inscriptions, announcing not only wealth but administrative confidence. A coin is more than money; it is authority made portable.

Aksum's reach was not merely commercial. It was political and sometimes military. Across the Red Sea, South Arabia was close enough to matter, and later Aksumite interventions there show that the sea was not a barrier but a bridge. When you control harbors and ships, water becomes a corridor of influence.

But Aksum also reminds us of a broader African truth: states grow when they can tax movement. Whether that movement is caravans crossing a desert or ships crossing a strait, the logic is the same. Revenue funds armies. Armies secure routes. Secured routes attract merchants. Merchants create wealth worth taxing. The cycle tightens.

Now turn west, away from the Red Sea, into the long interior where the Sahara is not an emptiness but a filter.

The **Niger bend**—where the Niger River curves through what is now Mali—would later become famous for cities like Timbuktu and Gao in the medieval era. But the foundations of river-based urbanism begin earlier, with settlements that grew where water, pasture, and trade met. River corridors made movement easier than overland travel in many seasons. They also allowed agriculture and fishing to support dense populations. Where density rises, markets rise; where markets rise, authority tends to consolidate.

In this early phase, we do not have the kind of written archives that survive in the Mediterranean world. Much of the evidence comes from archaeology: settlement patterns, material remains, traces of craft production and exchange. That absence of text is not absence of history. It simply means the story is told through soil, pottery, and the quiet logic of where people chose to live.

Picture again the market in a river town. A trader arrives from farther upstream with fish dried hard as wood. Another arrives from inland with animal skins. Someone brings copper or iron objects that are valuable not only as tools but as status items. Salt—so crucial for diet and preservation—moves through networks that may stretch toward desert edges. People in such markets are not thinking in terms of "West Africa" as a category. They are thinking in terms of trust: who delivers reliably, who cheats, who pays debts, who can be relied on when the river floods or fails.

These river towns are early signs of a world that will later produce larger states and cities. The beginnings matter because they show how urbanism can rise not only around temples or palaces but around exchange—the daily need to trade and the political need to manage that trade.

Now shift south and east, into one of the most consequential movements in African history: the **Bantu expansions**.

The phrase can mislead if it suggests a single migration wave like an invading army. It was not that. It was a long, complex set of movements and cultural-linguistic spread, unfolding over many centuries, beginning earlier than our chapter's time frame and continuing through late antiquity and beyond. Bantu-speaking communities expanded from parts of West/Central Africa into eastern and southern Africa, carrying languages, farming practices, and ironworking knowledge—though the details varied by region and scholars debate timing and mechanisms.

What drove such movement? Not one cause. A mix: population growth in some areas, the search for new farmland, the opportunities created by new crops and technologies, ecological shifts, and the simple human logic that if a frontier is open and resources are available, people will move into it. Along the way, Bantu-speaking groups interacted with other communities—hunter-gatherers, pastoralists—through exchange, intermarriage, competition, and sometimes conflict. The result was not cultural replacement in every case. It was cultural transformation: new blends, new identities, new social landscapes.

Iron sits at the center of that transformation, not as a "magic" technology, but as a practical multiplier.

In a small clearing near a village, the ground is blackened where a furnace has burned. Charcoal dust clings to hands and forearms. A bellows wheezes. A worker's face shines with sweat as he feeds air into the heat. Inside, ore is turning into something usable, something that changes what people can do: sharper tools for clearing land, hoes for farming, axes for wood, spearheads for defense and hunting.

This is ironworking as a social act. It requires knowledge, fuel, labor coordination, and often ritual attention, because a furnace feels like a living thing when you stand beside it.

Communities that can produce iron can expand agriculture, increase surplus, and defend territory more effectively. That does not automatically create states, but it creates the conditions in which bigger, more organized communities become feasible.

As Bantu-speaking communities moved, they helped spread such capabilities across wide regions. The growth of farming and ironworking supported larger settlements and more complex social organization, especially when combined with local ecological advantages—fertile soils, reliable water, productive pasturelands.

Now turn back to the coast, where Africa's expanding worlds began to face the Indian Ocean more directly.

Along the **East African** shoreline, from the Horn down toward modern Tanzania and beyond, coastal communities were forming that would later become the **Swahili** world. In this early period—roughly the first centuries CE into late antiquity—settlements grew around fishing, farming, and trade. Their material record includes something small but telling: **coastal trade beads**.

Beads are easy to underestimate. They are light, durable, and emotionally powerful. They can be jewelry, currency, status, ritual objects. And they travel well. When archaeologists find glass beads far from their production origins, they are finding the fingerprints of long-distance trade.

On a sandy street near a shoreline, a trader opens a pouch. Beads spill into his palm—blue, green, translucent, some with tiny imperfections that catch the light. Local people gather, not because beads are "trinkets," but because beads can be wealth made visible, wearable, exchangeable. They can mark marriage alliances. They can signal connection to faraway goods and faraway prestige.

The presence of such beads tells us that East African coastal communities were already plugged into Indian Ocean networks that linked Arabia, Persia, South Asia, and beyond. They were not passive recipients. Coastal settlements supplied goods—ivory, animal products, perhaps slaves in some contexts, timber, resins—and they offered ports, water, food, and brokerage. Traders needed local knowledge. Monsoon sailing requires predictable stops. The coast, therefore, became a chain of nodes, and over time those nodes developed distinctive urban and cultural forms.

This is the beginning of a world in which Islam, arriving later, will find ready-made trade corridors and multilingual coastal societies.

But even before Islam's rise, the Swahili coast was already learning to live as an interface: African inland goods meeting oceanic exchange, local languages meeting merchant tongues, coastal identities forming in the overlap.

So Africa's expanding worlds in this era are not one story but several interconnected ones:

In the northeast, Aksum builds a highland-to-sea state that leverages Red Sea trade and projects influence across water. In the west, river corridors like the Niger bend nurture early urban nodes where exchange and ecology support growing settlement complexity. Across central, eastern, and southern regions, Bantu-speaking expansions spread languages and productive systems, often alongside ironworking, reshaping demographics and social organization. On the eastern coast, early Swahili settlements begin to turn the Indian Ocean into a source of wealth and cultural connection, marked in the archaeological record by imported beads and traded goods.

These networks do more than move commodities. They move techniques, social norms, and ways of organizing life.

Ironworking changes what land can become. River markets change what communities can sustain. Sea trade changes what coastal towns can imagine, because it brings the outside world into daily bargaining. And states like Aksum show that Africa can anchor international corridors, not merely supply them.

Return to the river town market where we began. As afternoon turns toward evening, the crowd thins. Canoes push off with lighter loads and heavier news. Someone has heard about fighting in a distant region. Someone mentions a drought upstream. Someone carries a rumor about a new coin, a new ruler, a new tax demanded at the next crossing.

In the forge, the furnace cools, leaving behind slag and a few precious blooms of metal. In a coastal settlement, a child strings beads onto fiber thread while an elder watches the horizon for sails.

Africa in this era is not waiting for history to arrive. History is already traveling through it—by river, by roadless paths, by coastline, by the disciplined heat of iron.

33

The Classic Americas

The stone is still wet where the rain ran over it an hour ago. A scribe stands close enough to smell the limestone—chalky, sharp—while he traces the carved grooves with his fingertips, checking that the lines are clean. Above him, the stela rises like a frozen shout: a ruler in elaborate headdress, feet planted on a symbolic earth, hands holding the signs of office. Below the image, rows of glyphs record what must not be forgotten: a date, a lineage claim, a victory, a dedication.

People gather as the clouds thin. Someone murmurs the count aloud, not because everyone can read, but because everyone knows that time itself is political. The calendar is not a neutral tool; it is the ruler's proof that the city's life fits into cosmic order. The stela does not merely commemorate. It commands memory.

This is the Classic Americas at full voice—cities rising in forests and valleys, empires spreading through mountain corridors, landscapes engineered into farms and roads, authority enacted through ritual and recorded in stone and earth.

Between roughly **250 and 900 CE** in Mesoamerica—the period often called the **Classic**—and during overlapping centuries in the Andes, American societies built political forms that were both intensely local and profoundly interconnected. They did not need Eurasian technologies to do it. They needed organized labor, agricultural systems that could sustain dense populations, and legitimacy frameworks strong enough to bind people to rulers in environments that could be generous one year and punishing the next.

Begin in the Maya lowlands, where cities grew in a landscape that asked hard questions of water and coordination.

The Classic Maya world was not one kingdom. It was a mosaic of **city-states**, each with its own dynasty, its own emblem glyphs, its own alliances and rivalries. Cities like **Tikal**, **Calakmul**, **Palenque**, **Copán**, and many others competed for prestige and control. Politics was personal and dynastic, but it was also institutional. Kingship was not simply power. It was a role performed through ceremony, warfare, marriage alliances, and monumental building.

The stela inscription is how a Maya king fought the most important battle of all: the battle against forgetting.

A Maya ruler's legitimacy depended on lineage—who his ancestors were, which gods favored the dynasty, which victories proved divine support. Stelae and temple inscriptions recorded "accession" dates, ritual events, captive-taking, alliances, and the names of rivals. The Maya **Long Count** calendar allowed rulers to anchor events in deep time with astonishing precision, reaching back to mythic beginnings. By placing themselves in that cosmic timeline, kings made a claim that was both political and metaphysical: my rule is not an accident of force; it is part of the universe's order.

But Classic Maya politics was not only about ceremony. It was also about war.

Maya warfare often focused on capturing elites, controlling trade routes, and forcing tribute or allegiance rather than annihilating populations. Cities rose and fell through shifting alliances. A powerful king could dominate neighbors for a generation, then see influence collapse after a defeat, a succession dispute, or a drought that shook agricultural security. The political map was restless.

And above that restlessness hovered a question that shaped Classic Maya history: how connected were these cities to forces beyond the Maya world?

One answer stands out in the highlands of central Mexico: **Teotihuacan**.

Teotihuacan, near modern Mexico City, reached its height roughly between **100 and 550 CE**. It was one of the largest cities in the world at its peak, laid out on a grand grid with monumental avenues and pyramids that still command the landscape. We do not fully know how Teotihuacan was governed—whether by kings, councils, or other structures—because its texts are not as legible as Maya inscriptions. But its influence is unmistakable in material culture and in the political tremors it sent outward.

Teotihuacan's presence in Maya politics is one of the Classic period's most dramatic interregional stories.

In **378 CE**, a figure known from Maya texts as **Siyaj K'ak'** ("Fire is Born") arrived at **Tikal**—an event recorded in inscriptions with a specificity that makes it feel like a door slamming. The same day, Tikal's king died, and soon a new regime aligned with Teotihuacan-style imagery and possibly Teotihuacan-linked patrons took power. Scholars debate the exact nature of Teotihuacan's role—direct conquest, strategic intervention, alliance backed by force—but the pattern suggests something more than cultural admiration. It suggests power projected across hundreds of kilometers.

Teotihuacan influence appears in Maya art and architecture—warrior imagery, certain weapon styles, and diplomatic symbolism. It also appears in the logic of politics: connections to Teotihuacan could enhance legitimacy and intimidate rivals. In a world of competing city-states, being linked to a distant, powerful metropolis was a political asset.

So Classic Mesoamerica was not a set of isolated jungles cities. It was a networked arena where trade routes, diplomatic missions, and ideological signals moved between regions. Obsidian, jade, cacao, feathers, salt—these were not just goods. They were leverage.

Now shift south to the Andes, where another kind of Classic-era transformation unfolded—less centered on dynastic inscriptions, more on territorial organization and state infrastructure.

In the central Andes, the **Middle Horizon** period (often dated roughly **600–1000 CE**) saw the rise of large states that projected influence across wide regions: **Wari** and **Tiwanaku**.

The **Wari** state, centered in the highlands near modern Ayacucho in Peru, developed a networked form of imperial influence. Wari established administrative centers, spread distinctive architectural styles, and likely managed resources and labor through systems that allowed coordination across varied ecological zones. Unlike Maya polities, Wari authority is not primarily recorded through long dynastic texts. It is visible in settlement patterns, road-like corridors, storage facilities, and the spread of standardized state aesthetics.

Tiwanaku, centered near Lake Titicaca (in what is now Bolivia), built power in a high-altitude environment that demands agricultural ingenuity. Tiwanaku society is associated with monumental stone architecture and a distinctive religious iconography that spread widely. Its influence reached into multiple valleys and regions, partly through trade and colonization, partly through religious prestige.

And what made such Andean states possible was not only ideology or military force. It was land and water engineering on a grand scale.

Terraced farming is where imperial power becomes visible in soil. A hillside has been cut into steps—stone retaining walls holding back earth, creating flat plots that capture water and resist erosion. From above, terraces look like a patterned cloth laid over the mountains. From within, they feel like a miracle of patience. Each step is labor, and each step is a promise: we will control enough food to feed specialists, armies, builders, and priests. We will make the mountain serve the community.

Terraces also support another Andean strategy: production across vertical ecological zones. In the Andes, a few kilometers can mean a change in climate, crops, and pasture. States that could organize labor across these zones could buffer risk and accumulate surplus. They could move maize, potatoes, quinoa, dried meat, textiles, and other goods between zones in planned flows, turning ecological diversity into political strength.

Roads, too, mattered—routes across highlands and valleys that allowed state agents, goods, and messages to move. Later, the Inca would build the most famous Andean road system, but earlier states laid groundwork in the logic of connectivity: administrative centers linked by corridors, storage nodes, and communities tied into labor obligations.

This is where the long-distance messenger belongs. He runs, not in a straight line like a Roman road would allow, but along mountain paths where every turn is a decision. He carries a small bundle—perhaps a message in knotted cords, a token, a verbal memorandum he has memorized with disciplined repetition. His body is lean from constant motion, his lungs trained to thin air. He knows where the next rest station is, where fresh water can be found, which communities are obligated to provide food, which ones might be hostile if politics have shifted.

He is the living infrastructure of an empire. Without him, the center cannot know the periphery. Without him, orders travel too slowly to matter. With him, distance becomes manageable.

In both Mesoamerica and the Andes, ritual authority remained central, but it took different shapes.

In the Maya world, kingship was deeply theatrical and genealogical, anchored in calendars and monumental texts. Ritual performance—bloodletting, offerings, public ceremonies—tied rulers to gods and ancestors. In the Andean world, state religion often emphasized broad iconographic systems that could unify diverse regions under shared sacred imagery. Tiwanaku's religious symbols, for example, could travel with crafts and architecture, creating a sense of belonging to a larger sacred order. Wari's spread of standardized aesthetics suggests a similar impulse: use shared forms to bind a wide realm.

Ritual is not a distraction from "real" politics. It is one of the ways politics becomes real for people who cannot see the palace every day.

And across these worlds, landscape management was the silent partner of authority. Reservoirs, terraces, canals, causeways, and planned cities were not only practical solutions. They were proofs of competence. A ruler who can mobilize labor to build a terrace system can likely mobilize labor for war. A state that can organize food storage can support administrators. A city that can schedule rituals by calendar can schedule taxes and corvée.

Yet these systems carried tensions. Cities and states depend on stable food systems. When droughts or climate shifts hit—when rainfall patterns change in the Maya lowlands, or when Andean ecological balance is disrupted—political legitimacy can fray. Because when a ruler claims cosmic order, people notice when the world feels disordered. The Classic Maya "collapse" in the southern lowlands after **c. 800–900 CE** is not a single event but a complex regional transformation involving drought stress, war, political fragmentation, and shifting trade routes. Some cities were abandoned. Others adapted. Northern centers continued. The point is not that Maya civilization "ended." It reconfigured.

Similarly, Wari and Tiwanaku influence waned by around the **tenth century**, and regions reorganized into new political forms. Here too, "collapse" is often a misleading word. People did not vanish. They shifted, rebuilt, and carried institutional memory forward.

Return to the stela. The rain has dried. The carved date remains. A ruler's name still catches light where the grooves shadow it. Even if the dynasty falls, the stone keeps speaking, because that was its purpose. It was built to outlast.

On a terrace, farmers check soil moisture with practiced hands, repairing walls where stones have slipped. A messenger runs again, breathing hard in thin air, carrying the state's memory in motion.

The Classic Americas were worlds where time was counted with fierce precision and landscapes were reshaped with patient force. They were complex not as echoes of Eurasia, but as parallel achievements—different materials, different animals, different paths, the same human problem: how to organize many lives into one political story.

34

The Sacred Order

The reed pen scratches softly against parchment, a sound so small it seems impossible that it could change the world. In the dim light of a scriptorium, a monk leans close to the page. The lamp's flame trembles when someone shifts nearby, and the shadows of hands and sleeves move across the desk like slow water. Ink smells metallic and sharp. The manuscript itself is expensive enough to feel like a crime to waste: animal skin stretched thin, scraped smooth, ruled with faint lines to keep the letters disciplined.

He copies carefully, not because he is trying to make art, but because errors multiply. A word missed here becomes a dispute there. A phrase altered becomes a heresy. His work is not only devotion; it is infrastructure. Each line is a plank laid across time, meant to carry a community that will never meet him.

Outside the monastery walls, people pray in many ways. In marketplaces and homes, faith mixes with local customs, old gods, protective charms, songs sung for healing. But inside, a different kind of project is underway: the slow consolidation of religion into institutions that can survive distance, persecution, and political change.

This is one of late antiquity's quiet revolutions. Empires fracture and reform. Borders shift. Yet religious communities—Christian, Buddhist, Jewish, and others—become more durable precisely because they learn how to store themselves: in scripture, in law, in monasteries, in pilgrimage routes, in disciplined habits of memory.

A religion becomes hard to erase once it can live in books, buildings, and routines. In the early centuries of these traditions, belief was often carried by people and stories—teachers traveling, communities meeting, rituals performed in particular places. That form is powerful, but fragile.

It depends on unbroken chains of memory. It is vulnerable to violence and dispersal. As the world became more connected—and more unstable—religions faced a question that was as practical as it was spiritual: how do we stay the same when we spread?

The answer, again and again, was text.

But "scripture" is not born complete. It is chosen.

Canon formation—the process by which certain texts are recognized as authoritative and others are not—is both a theological and a social act. It shapes what counts as truth, who gets to teach, and how a community decides disputes. It is never purely peaceful. When people disagree about God, or liberation, or law, they do not simply disagree in private. They form factions. They claim legitimacy. They accuse each other of betrayal. Canon formation is a way to make argument governable.

In the Christian world, by the fourth century, councils and bishops were increasingly involved in defining orthodoxy and rejecting certain teachings. Lists of accepted writings solidified over time, with regional variations and long debates. The exact chronology of when "the"

New Testament canon was fixed varies depending on how you define "fixed," but by late antiquity the broad shape had become widely recognized across major churches. This mattered not just for doctrine but for authority. A bishop could point to scripture. A preacher could claim continuity. A community could decide who was inside and outside the boundary of belief.

In Buddhism, canon formation took a different form, partly because Buddhism was already plural and expansive, with many schools and languages. Collections of teachings—the sutras and associated texts—were transmitted, translated, debated, and compiled. The growth of **Mahayana** scriptures in particular expanded the textual universe, and with it, the need for scholarly work: translation choices, commentaries, and institutional support for study. A Buddhist canon was not simply one set of books. It became a vast library, and that library needed places and people to maintain it.

In Judaism, scripture had long been central, but late antiquity saw intensified work of interpretation and legal codification that would become foundational for rabbinic communities. The Torah's authority was not simply read; it was argued into daily life, through legal reasoning and communal practice. Here, canon and law braided together: a text becomes living through interpretation and application.

In all these traditions, the same pattern appears: to persist across distance, you need agreed reference points—texts, rules, rituals—that can travel. And texts need caretakers. This is where monastic networks become so important—not as isolated spiritual retreats, but as organizations that knit together regions.

Monasteries are often imagined as places where people flee the world. In late antiquity, monasteries also held the world together. They preserved and produced manuscripts. They educated novices and sometimes laypeople. They provided charity, lodging, and medical care in some contexts. They hosted travelers, served as economic actors through landholding and production, and became political players when rulers needed moral legitimacy or when bishops needed organized support.

You can see the monastic network in its most literal form when a group of monks travels with a bundle of books. A pack animal carries a wooden chest wrapped against rain. Inside are texts copied by hand—rare, valuable, portable authority. The monks' sandals wear thin on roads that are not safe. They stop at other monasteries where hospitality is expected but not free; it is paid in prayers, news, or future support. They carry letters of recommendation. They carry knowledge of routes. A monastery, in this network, is a node: a place where faith is practiced, stored, and transmitted.

Monastic life also created an internal discipline that empires often envied. A community that can organize time—wake, pray, work, eat, study—can organize people. And organized people can become a power. That is why rulers patronized monasteries and also feared them. Patronage could buy prayers and legitimacy. But monasteries could also resist rulers, critique them, or shelter rebels. Sacred institutions are never purely submissive once they are strong.

Alongside monasteries, another network expanded: pilgrimage.

A pilgrimage road is a strange kind of highway. It is traveled by people who are not merchants and not soldiers, though they use the same inns and face the same bandits. Pilgrims move because place matters. A shrine, a relic, a holy mountain, a river crossing—these become points where the sacred feels closer, where forgiveness can be sought, where healing is hoped for, where vows are fulfilled.

Picture a pilgrimage road at dawn. Dust rises under feet. A family walks with a small bundle and a staff. An elderly man rides on a donkey, swaying with each step. Someone sings softly to keep pace. They pass roadside sellers offering bread, water, small amulets. A few pilgrims travel with money; many travel with only enough. They sleep in crowded spaces, share food, share stories, share fear. The road itself becomes a community.

Pilgrimage does something important: it makes religion visible and collective. It turns belief into movement. It creates shared experiences that can outlast doctrine disputes. It also spreads ideas, because pilgrims talk. They carry songs and stories back to their villages. They learn new rituals at shrines. They bring back objects—blessed cloth, sacred water, small icons—that anchor the experience in daily life.

Pilgrimage also produces economies: inns, markets, artisans, guides. Sacred geography becomes a source of wealth. Wealth attracts attention. Attention attracts regulation. And so religion becomes tied to administration again, sometimes in ways that deepen faith, sometimes in ways that corrupt it.

As religions spread, they did not travel as pure packages. They met local worlds. They adapted.

This is where syncretism—the blending of practices and symbols—becomes both inevitable and controversial.

A new religion enters a region with old gods, old festivals, old healing practices. People do not stop being who they were overnight. They map new saints onto old spirits. They reinterpret older rituals as compatible with the new faith. They keep charms because illness still terrifies them. They attend official services and also whisper to protective forces at home. Sometimes religious authorities tolerate this. Sometimes they condemn it. Sometimes they absorb it by renaming it.

Syncretism is often described as "mixing," but it is more precise to call it negotiation. It is what happens when communities try to make new meaning live inside old lives.

This negotiation is especially visible in the formation of law-and-ethics communities: groups defined not only by belief but by shared rules.

In late antiquity, many religions became increasingly concerned with discipline—what people eat, how they marry, how they inherit, what counts as sin, what counts as purity, what counts as justice. Rules do not only constrain. They also create belonging. If you live by a shared code, you recognize one another across distance.

Christian communities developed increasingly detailed norms through councils, bishops' letters, and evolving canon law traditions. These norms shaped marriage, clerical behavior, property disputes, and communal discipline. Jewish communities developed and refined legal interpretation through rabbinic authority, shaping daily life through rulings on everything from commerce to Sabbath practice. Buddhist monastic communities lived under vinaya rules that governed conduct, possessions, and communal decisions, creating a recognizable institutional life that could be replicated from monastery to monastery.

Law and ethics did something else: they made religion administratively useful.

A ruler does not only want people to believe. A ruler wants people to behave predictably. Religious codes can support public order, encourage charity, discourage certain kinds of violence, and create networks of authority that a state can use—or must contend with. This is why emperors like Constantine involved themselves in Christian disputes. This is why Sasanian kings watched religious communities carefully. This is why local rulers patronized monasteries and temples. Religion was no longer merely a personal matter. It was governance by other means.

Inside these institutions, debates could be fierce. A monastery courtyard, mid-afternoon. The sun turns dust into gold. Monks sit in a loose circle, robes rustling when they shift. A senior teacher asks a question that sounds simple: What is the nature of the self? How can compassion be universal if the world is full of harm? What does a scripture passage truly mean? A younger monk answers too quickly, eager to prove himself. Another interrupts, citing a different commentary. Voices rise, then quiet under a glance from the elder.

This is not fictional drama. It is an ordinary moment in communities that took ideas seriously because ideas shaped salvation, and salvation shaped authority. The debate is not only about truth. It is about which line of interpretation will be taught, which texts will be copied, which rituals will be performed, which leaders will gain influence.

And through such debates, traditions sharpened. Some beliefs were declared heretical. Some practices were standardized. Some local customs were tolerated under a new name. Some were fought like enemies. Over time, the boundaries of communities hardened, even as real lived religion remained messier than official rules.

That messiness is not a failure of religion. It is the normal condition of human life. People want both meaning and protection, both community and personal survival. They will hold contradictory practices in the same hand if it helps them endure.

So by the end of late antiquity, religions had become more than movements of believers. They had become systems.

Systems of texts—copied, translated, argued, and canonized.

Systems of institutions—monasteries, churches, rabbinic schools—capable of lasting through political upheaval.

Systems of movement—pilgrimage routes and networks of hospitality—linking distant places into shared sacred geographies.

Systems of law and ethics—codes that shaped daily life and created recognizable communities across distance.

Return to the monk copying manuscripts. His wrist aches. His eyes burn. He pauses, lifts the pen, and blows gently to dry the ink. Outside, the world remains unstable. A dynasty might change by next year. A frontier might shift. A tax might rise. A plague might return. But the text on his page will outlast all that if he does his work well.

That is the strange power of scripture and institution. They give a community a memory that does not depend on one city's walls or one king's life. They create a continuity that can pass through conquest and collapse without dissolving.

And as these religious systems harden and travel, a new force is about to enter the connected world with extraordinary speed: a revelation that will become empire, a community that will become a vast intellectual zone, and a network of trade and law that will reshape deserts, seas, and cities.

www.ingramcontent.com/pod-product-compliance
Lightning Source LLC
Chambersburg PA
CBHW050010170726
48282CB00025B/342
* 9 7 8 9 3 5 6 9 2 2 6 6 2 *